Stand Out
From the Crowd

SECRETS TO CRAFTING A WINNING COMPANY IDENTITY

JAY LIPE

KAPLAN PUBLISHING

This publication is designed to provide accurate and authoritative information in regard to the subject matter covered. It is sold with the understanding that neither the publisher nor the author is engaged in rendering legal, accounting, or other professional service. If legal advice or other expert assistance is required, the services of a competent professional should be sought.

President, Kaplan Publishing: Roy Lipner
Vice President and Publisher: Maureen McMahon
Acquisitions Editor: Karen Murphy
Development Editor: Trey Thoelcke
Senior Managing Editor: Jack Kiburz
Typesetter: Caitlin Ostrow
Cover Designer: Design Literate

Author's note: Every effort has been made to make this book as complete and accurate as possible. However, there *may* be typographical and/or content mistakes. Therefore, this text should be used only as a general guide and not as the definitive source. Furthermore, this book contains information on marketing that is current only up to the printing date.

Printed in the United States of America

06 07 08 10 9 8 7 6 5 4 3 2 1

Library of Congress Cataloging-in-Publication Data

Lipe, Jay B.
  Stand out from the crowd : secrets to crafting a winning company identity / Jay Lipe.
      p. cm.
  Includes bibliographical references and index.
  ISBN-13: 978-1-4195-2300-7
  ISBN-10: 1-4195-2300-7
  1. Corporate image. 2. Marketing—Management. I. Title.
  HD59.2.L57 2006
  659.2–dc22
                                                        2006010543

DEDICATION

Dedicated to My Family

My wife, "Bin"; our daughter, "Chammer"; our son, "lil' Buddy"; my mom, Joan Lipe; dad, Jay A. Lipe; stepmom, Bonnie; brother, Jeff; and sister, Katie.

To the rest of our family, looking down from above, and to God, for being the lamp to my feet.

I'd also like to thank all my clients. Hopefully, I taught you as much as I learned.

C o n t e n t s

s there really a need for another marketing book? You bet there is. Today's lightning-fast pace, cutthroat competition, and ever-expanding marketing knowledge has elevated marketing to *the* most important skill for business leaders today. I don't care if your product (or service) is hands down the best on the market; without sound marketing in place, it won't get far.

During my speeches and seminars, I'm often asked, "Which marketing program, dollar for dollar, gives my company the biggest bang for the buck? A direct-mail program? Networking? Cold calling? Pay-per-click?" My answer is always the same: *A standout company identity*. Sure, you can pour money and time into a direct-mail, telemarketing, personal selling, or online marketing effort, but once you convince a prospect to contact your company directly, he or she will experience your company identity firsthand. If, at this point, the strategic thinking behind your marketing is flawed, or your marketing tools craft the wrong image, the buyer will go away—never to return. Game over.

Think of your company identity as the foundation—the very bedrock—on which all the rest of your company's marketing efforts will sit. If this foundation, your identity, is slapped together quickly, inconsistently assembled, or poorly constructed, what chance will the rest of your marketing have? Lest you think I'm blowing this out of proportion, take a look at this list of warning signs for a poor company identity. See if any of them apply to your company:

Top Ten Warning Signs Your Company Identity Needs Help

10. Every one of your marketing materials looks different from the others.
9. You have to repeat your company name, maybe sometimes even spelling it out.
8. You spend the majority of any meeting with a buyer explaining what you do.
7. Prospects would rather talk about your competitor.
6. When asked what makes your company unique, the room gets quiet.
5. Your Web site has been "under construction" for more than six months.
4. Your heart races when someone says, "Tell me about your company."

3. The most common comment about your company's visual identity is "I don't get it."

2. You're hesitant to pass out company literature because of the image it portrays.

1. It's been years since you've hired an outside marketing vendor.

If, after reading these statements, you said to yourself, "That describes us," you owe it to your company to keep reading. If you chuckled as you read this list because you were reminded of a good friend's company, keep reading.

I wrote this book for Fortune 500 executives, midlevel business leaders, and owners of small businesses. You may think that's overambitious—taking on too many audiences at once. But after working 20+ years with all three audiences, consulting directly with hundreds of clients, and addressing thousands more through my speeches and seminars, I've learned that *all three* groups fall short of crafting a winning company identity.

Another thing is clear to me: the longer these people delay improving their company identity, the further behind they'll fall. And one day, in the not-too-distant future, a more successful competitor of theirs (who just happens to have developed a highly professional, solidly consistent identity) will come calling . . . to buy their company. And at that point, the game *is* over.

WHY YOUR COMPANY NEEDS A WELL-CRAFTED IDENTITY

1

WHY HAVING A STANDOUT COMPANY IDENTITY IS SO IMPORTANT

The dogmas of the quiet past are inadequate to the stormy present.

ABRAHAM LINCOLN

The most powerful marketing tool for any company today is a standout company identity. Think about each of these scenarios for a moment:

- Your e-commerce company's Web site features the largest selection of high-quality products in your category, yet the home page takes more than a minute to download and the rest of the site is extremely difficult to navigate. Will your company succeed?
- Your company has developed a world-class service in the travel industry, yet your logo is cheesy, your brochure shrieks amateurish, and your business cards are printed on an inkjet printer (and half of them have smudges). Will your company succeed?
- Your software business has developed a very successful lead-generation campaign that drives buyers to call your company, yet the first voice they hear is

a short-tempered receptionist who lashes out for no reason and has a disconcerting habit of disconnecting callers. Will your company succeed?

Will any of these companies thrive? Probably not. That's because in each of these scenarios, the companies didn't have a standout company identity to back up their efforts. And these days, in our hypercompetitive world, buyers who sense a lack of professionalism can easily find a handful of your competitors in seconds.

Don't undermine your company's efforts to succeed by shooting yourself in the foot with a slapdash company identity. If you forsake developing a truly professional and consistent brand identity for your company, your buyers will

- experience doubt about your company,
- be confused about what you do,
- fail to understand how your company helps them,
- be indecisive about doing business with you,
- distrust what your company says, and
- perceive a gulf between what your company *says* it does and what it does.

In short, establishing a standout identity is the very foundation for any company's marketing effort. With a standout identity in place, your company will earn trust faster, benefit from positive word of mouth, enjoy frequent referrals, attract larger numbers of buyers, craft a more professional image, grow awareness faster, and motivate buyers to take action quickly.

It hasn't always been this way. As recently as just 20 years ago, companies could portray a subpar brand for their company yet still register sales increases. But times have changed. Buyers are far more sophisticated, and a host of other factors have converged, demanding that every company present a professional and consistent brand identity. The coldhearted reality is that developing a standout company identity is no longer an option for success in today's market—it's a requirement.

TECHNOLOGY'S EXPONENTIAL RISE

Over the past 40 years, technology has transformed almost every facet of our society. Dating back to 1975 when the first personal computer with a microprocessor was introduced *(Quick, what was the brand? Answer: the Altair 8800),* this wave of technology has engulfed the marketing field and sparked widespread changes in the way companies market themselves. To put this in proper perspective, consider the world in 1975:

- Microsoft Corporation was just opening its doors (1975).
- E-mail, invented in 1972, was celebrating its third birthday.
- Cell phones had been introduced but were just two years old.
- Voice mail was still seven years away from becoming a reality (1982).
- The Internet was nine years away from being named (1984).

But contrast this with today's digitized world:

- There are almost 1 *billion* televisions around the world.
- The average television in a U.S. household offers more than 90 channels.
- Desktop computers today put more computing power in the hands of a consumer than the U.S. government first used to *send men to the moon*.
- More than 31 million domain names, 200 million IP hosts, and 840 million Internet users exist worldwide.
- It took only four years for the Internet to enjoy an audience of 50 million users—a feat radio and television needed 38 and 13 years to accomplish, respectively.

Not only has this digital revolution changed the way we receive information, it has forever altered the landscape of marketing by spawning a host of brand-new digital marketing tools.

A MARKETING TOOL KIT THAT'S BURSTING AT THE SEAMS

One upshot of the digital revolution is that it has substantially increased the number of marketing tools that compete for a buyer's attention. Just look at some of the new tools the Internet has produced:

- E-newsletters
- Search engine optimization
- Pay-per-click advertising
- Directory listings
- Link-building campaigns
- Live chat
- Discussion forums
- Rich media ads
- Pop-up ads
- Blogs

- Internet publicity campaigns
- Banner advertising
- Affiliate marketing
- Viral marketing efforts
- Autoresponders

And why stop there? As the digital revolution sparked new tools, the off-line world was not far behind. New off-line marketing tools that have come into vogue are:

- Buzz marketing
- PR stunts
- Viral marketing
- Street stenciling
- Mobile video trucks
- Video projection billboards
- Coffee-sleeve advertising
- Golf cart advertising
- Digital indoor media
- Product placement
- Product seeding
- Rip-away wild posters
- Elevator video screens
- Graffiti performances
- Ambush marketing
- Nightlife product sampling
- Branded bar bathrooms
- Retail shopping-bag ads

These days, virtually everywhere we turn, there is an ad. As a result, consumers today are headed towards a saturation point—or what I call *ad overload*.

AD OVERLOAD

As a teenager in the 1970s, I was exposed to, on average, about 500 marketing messages a day. Today, my teenage children are exposed to, by some official estimates, 10 times that amount, or roughly 5,000 marketing messages a day. Consider just one marketing medium—television advertising. In 1965, television commercials averaged 53 seconds in length. Today, they are just 25 seconds. This means that, on average, for every hour of television we watch, we're bombarded by close to twice as many commercials as we were as kids.

On the Internet, a majority (54 percent in 2005) of wired U.S. households are now using a broadband connection, up from near zero a decade ago. As a result, Web surfers can now receive content (and advertisements) up to 40 times faster than they could using a dial-up connection.

Let's not forget the impact multitasking has on this promotional barrage. According to BIGresearch's 2004 Simultaneous Media Survey, 65 percent of all people watching TV are also checking the mail, 60 percent are online, 55 percent are reading the newspaper, and 52 percent are perusing magazines. Because these numbers don't add up to 100 percent, we can reasonably assume that many consumers are using three or more media simultaneously. Three times the media means roughly three times the number of ads.

AD OVERLOAD STARTS AT AN EARLIER AGE

Just as significant as the increasing number of ads is how early in life we are exposed to this overload. In the United States, a typical first grader can name more than 200 brands. By the time a child in the United Kingdom reaches the age of 18, he or she has been exposed to 140,000 television commercials. You be the judge whether it has gotten out of hand: One mom-to-be in suburban Philadelphia, hoping to cash in on her first child's arrival, recently invited advertisers to place their names and logos on her baby's goods and clothing. One New York couple even attempted to auction off naming rights to their son for $500,000. There were no takers.

THE RISING TIDE OF COMPETITION

Ad overload aside, business owners must also contend with a feeding frenzy of competition. There are currently more than 23 million businesses in the United States, and every year an additional 570,000 new businesses are created. Almost 50 percent of these new businesses remain open after four years—a fact that generally never gets reported in today's media.

The global marketplace is now very real. Owing to the widespread adoption of the Internet and falling trade barriers, a glut of new competitors has entered the marketplace—your marketplace—in just the past decade. Particularly distressing is the fact that many of these competitors are now only a mouse click away for *your* buyers.

Evidence of this rising tide of competition can be easily found by examining the new century's Twin Tigers: China and India.

Take a look at these startling statistics that show just how important these two countries will become in the world market:

- In 1950, China didn't have a single city with a population of five million or more. By 2015, it will have *six* (Shenyang, Beijing, Tianjin, Chongqing, Wuhan, and Shanghai).
- In 1950, India also lacked a city with a population of five million or more. By 2015, it will have *five* (Mumbai/Bombay, Kolkata/Calcutta, Bangalore, Ahmadabad, and Delhi). As a point of comparison, in 1950 the United States had one city with a population of five million: New York. In 2015, it will have *three:* New York, Chicago, and Los Angeles.
- China's trade with the world (imports plus exports) rose 310 percent to US$1.2 trillion over the past ten years.
- Two-way trade between India and the United States in 2000 totaled $14.35 billion, a nearly 100 percent increase since 1993. Software exports from India to the United States accounted for an additional $3.5 billion in 2000.

Businesses around the globe now face a host of competitors that didn't exist a short decade ago, and it's safe to say that the level of competition is rising faster than a kite on a windy day.

A RISE IN MENTAL HORSEPOWER

In addition to this unprecedented rise in competition, or perhaps because of it, the business world is collectively becoming smarter about marketing. U.S. business schools churn out more than 112,000 freshly minted MBAs each year, and a large portion of these major in marketing.

Furthermore, recent data from the Global MBA Graduate Survey indicates that close to 40 percent of the 2005 class of MBA schools across the world are citizens from countries outside of the United States. Clearly, more and more worldwide businesses are benefiting from graduate-level marketing educations and applying that knowledge in the marketplace.

PREDICTIONS FOR OUR MARKETING FUTURE

Predicting the future is tricky; no one can accurately anticipate every development. But given recent changes in marketing, I think I can safely make the following predictions.

Choices for Consumers Will Continue to Mushroom

In their book *Differentiate or Die,* Jack Trout and Steve Rivkin make a strong case for how an increasing number of product choices have begun to paralyze consumers. As Figure 1.1 shows, buyers these days face a mind-numbing number of choices—each of which must be promoted and marketed to the masses.

Competitive Pressures Will Grow

Whether your company has been in business for 30 years or 30 minutes, you have competition. And even more competitors will enter your market in the years ahead. As your waters churn with more competitors each day, your company will be forced to differentiate or die.

FIGURE 1.1 *The Explosion of Choice*

Product Category	# of Choices in Early 1970s	# of Choices by Late 1990s
Software titles	0	250,000
Radio stations	7,038	12,458
Amusement parks	362	1,174
Community colleges	886	1,742
Breakfast cereals	160	340
Running shoe styles	5	285
Magazine titles	339	790
Bottled water brands	16	50
Mouthwashes	15	66

Source: *Differentiate or Die* by Jack Trout with Steve Rivkin (Wiley, 2000).

Your Company's Identity Must Be Crystal Clear to Cut Through the Clutter

In the midst of so much competition, the burning question on the minds of many company leaders I meet with is, "How do I make my company stand out?" And my answer is always the same: *Focus first on crafting a powerful company identity.* A powerful identity helps any company

- improve awareness,
- generate more recognition,
- build trust with its buyers,
- gain a competitive advantage, and
- close business faster.

All other aspects of marketing your business should be relegated to the back burner until this critical component is in place. With a compelling company identity in place, you can feel confident that any interaction a buyer has with your company—brought on by any of the various lead-generation efforts—will reinforce your company's brand image, allowing you to seal the deal again and again.

THE FIVE FACETS OF A STANDOUT COMPANY IDENTITY

There are five facets that every company identity stems from. For any company's identity to stand out from the crowd, it must deliver on all five facets—strategic factors, market touchpoints, written words, tried-and-true identity tools, and follow-through. (See Figure 1.2.) If your company can leverage each of these and present the highest quality company image, it will stand out. Without clear and focused attention to these five facets, however, your company image likely will come across as confused and unprofessional to your buyers.

Whatever the symptoms, the cure is clear: build a strong company identity. Whether your company has 20,000 employees or is just you in your home office, a well-crafted company identity creates

- higher awareness levels,
- stronger credibility,
- more trust,
- more leads,
- higher revenues and volumes,

FIGURE 1.2 *The Five Facets of Standout Company Identities*

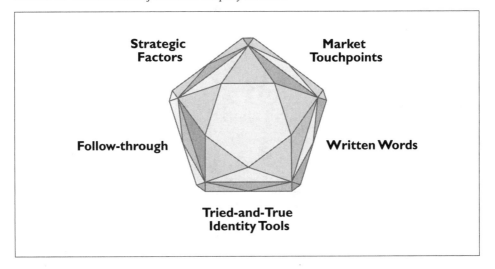

- more loyal customers,
- lower marketing expenses, and
- higher returns on investment.

CHAPTER WRAP

The only factor becoming scarce in a world of abundance is human attention.

KEVIN KELLY

Cluttered. Frenzied. Unpredictable. These are all words I use to describe today's marketing environment. But don't give up hope. The one surefire marketing vehicle that offers security and hope is a standout identity for your company.

Remember that in today's world, marketing isn't a luxury, it's a necessity. Increasingly, companies must market themselves just to survive, let alone thrive. But if any marketing effort is to be successful, it must first draw on the strength of its company identity.

2

THE TEN COMMANDMENTS FOR A WINNING COMPANY IDENTITY

Marketing is not an event, but a process. It has a beginning, a middle, but never an end, for it is a process. You improve it, perfect it, change it, even pause it. But you never stop it completely.

JAY CONRAD LEVINSON

Okay, these Ten Commandments didn't come from the mountain. And they're not carved on clay tablets. Yet any marketer worth his or her salt must follow these commandments to reach the promised land.

I. THOU SHALL HONOR EACH TOUCHPOINT

Every interaction your company has with a buyer is called a *touchpoint*. These touchpoints are defining moments of truth; each one is responsible for indelibly crafting your identity. From a company Web site, which might be the first thing a buyer sees, to the delivery person, whose brake lights may be the last, every single touchpoint between your company and its market adds to your buyer's storehouse of knowledge about your company identity.

To capitalize on these moments of truth and to present the strongest company identity possible, identify all your company's touchpoints and then work hard to improve each one. Here's a list of the more common touchpoints for any company. Take a minute to peruse the list in Figure 2.1, then note which ones are important touchpoints for your company.

Go through this list and determine which of these are your company's highest priority touchpoints—those that occur most frequently and also those that move buyers further along in the purchasing process. Let me give you an example.

FIGURE 2.1 *The Most Common Marketing Touchpoints*

Support staff marketing
☐ Receptionists
☐ Service departments
☐ Help desk(s)

Course-of-business marketing
☐ Invoices
☐ E-mail signature files
☐ Voice mail greetings
☐ On-hold messaging
☐ Packaging
☐ Delivery vehicles
☐ Company cars
☐ Appointment scheduling
☐ On-hold marketing

Sales channel marketing
☐ Presentations
☐ Estimates and quotes
☐ Proposals
☐ Contracts
☐ Pitch books

Print marketing
☐ Direct mail
☐ Advertisements
☐ Publicity articles
☐ Brochures
☐ Directory listings

In-person marketing
☐ Sales calls
☐ Networking
☐ Trade show booths
☐ Speaking engagements
☐ Service calls
☐ Delivery personnel
☐ Word-of-mouth mentions

Online marketing
☐ Web sites
☐ Micro-Web sites
☐ Landing pages
☐ Auto responders
☐ E-newsletters

Facilities marketing
☐ Storefronts
☐ Company signage
☐ Office interiors
☐ Conference rooms
☐ Store displays
☐ Point-of-purchase displays
☐ Store music
☐ Smells and fragrances

Other
☐ Sending faxes
☐ Logo wear
☐ Premiums (pens, etc.)
☐ Uniforms
☐ Thank-you notes

One spring, I was hired by a major travel agency to identify its high-five touch-points. To identify these for this agency, we conducted a survey with its top travel-ers. As part of this research, I literally had travelers walk me, step-by-step, through the exact process they used to gather information, and then book, their latest vaca-tion. I soon discovered a pattern. What we learned from this research was that the travel agency's high-five touchpoints were:

1. *Ads in the Sunday travel section of the local newspaper.* The travel section of the Sunday newspaper commands a very high readership. These readers turn to this section weekly to learn more about destinations, certain travel vendors, and special offers. Not only did we hear this from the respondents we surveyed, we also saw that whenever we didn't run an ad in the Sunday travel section, our phone calls the following day dropped drastically.

2. *The company's Web site.* After readers perused the Sunday travel ads, they invariably checked out a travel company's Web site for more information. As a result, we realized that every single ad we placed had to prominently feature the company's URL (Web site address).

3. *The receptionist.* After a traveler had viewed our ads and Web site, he or she very likely picked up the phone and called the agency to talk to an agent. The very first person this caller spoke with was our receptionist. During this call, the receptionist had two objectives: (1) Make the caller feel wel-come and (2) Determine which agent could best help the caller.

4. *The first conversation between the agent and the caller.* When the caller first made live contact with an agent, this was a critical touchpoint for the agency. With a line of attentive questioning and a warm tone, the agent could more often than not book the trip. Without either, the caller would likely hang up and dial one of our competitors. Keep in mind, this caller probably had the Sunday travel section in front of her when she called us, and that section had our competitors' ads listed right next to ours. Because of this, the first conversation between the agent and the caller had to go well.

5. *A "welcome home" contact by the agent.* Every top-selling agent at this $3 mil-lion company made a point to carve out time to call their clients immedi-ately after they returned home from a trip. During this call, the agent made sure the arrangements were acceptable, and then asked for refer-rals. This call was very important for several reasons. First, it served as a type of market research for the agent who had booked the trip; she could

learn firsthand about the airline trip and accommodations for future use with other travelers. But more important, this was the best time to ask the client for a referral. Satisfied travelers who had just returned from a great vacation were more apt to provide referrals, or, in the odd instance, book another trip.

Once we identified this company's high-five touchpoints, we set about improving them. Some required graphic design help (the ads and Web site), while others involved training efforts (the receptionist contact and agent calls). The main point is that all your company's touchpoints are important to its identity, but some are more important than others. Find out what they are, then work to continuously improve them.

II. THINE IDENTITY MUST BE CONSISTENT

Here's a challenge: the next time you have a minute, spread these basic company identity tools across a table:

- Business cards
- Letterhead
- Envelopes
- Your brochure, and
- Your Web site (have this up on a screen)

Now ask yourself this: how consistent is your company's identity across all these elements? Do you see the same brand images? Are the colors consistent? Do you see the identical typestyles? Are the same key messages found in both your brochure and on your Web site?

If just one of these tools isn't consistent with the others, you'll plant a seed of doubt in buyers' minds. They might say to themselves, "I liked this company up until I saw its cheesy brochure" or "I only started having questions after I saw the Web site."

To get buyers to trust your company, make consistency a hallmark of your company identity. With it, your company will enjoy:

- stronger brand recognition,
- clearer expectations for your branded product or service,
- a more professional image,
- greater differentiation from your competition, and
- a brand that is more highly valued.

To see how far a company goes to ensure consistency in its identity, visit the Wedgwood Company *(http://www.wedgwoodusa.com)*. This savvy company has standardized the consistency of its brand across its retail, direct-mail, and Internet channels. It insists on using the same type fonts, colors for border and background shading (blue), and styling across its catalog, stores, and Web site.

III. THOU SHALL ALWAYS HONOR YOUR PROMISES

Too many companies these days speak loudly yet carry a teeny-weeny stick. By this I mean that some marketers fancy themselves as carnival barkers and use phrases such as "Best in the universe" or "No one does it better than us." This kind of over-the-top copy does more harm than good to your company's identity. Rational people will see right through these claims and will develop suspicions about your company's character. Over time, continuous hype like this slowly chips away at your company's credibility.

Watts Wacker, the well-known futurist, once said that "A brand is a promise and in the end, you have to keep your promises." Remember that the words, statements, and claims you use in your company's communications also create promises for your company. Be true. Be authentic. Don't hype. If you do, and your words are found to be false, you'll forever be seen as a huckster.

IV. THOU SHALT NOT LACK FOCUS

We've all met unfocused people. One day this person boldly announces a brand-new obsession (e.g., rock climbing). He dives headlong into this new fixation, outfitting himself with the latest gadgets and proudly spouting its jargon. Just when you think he has found a passion (and focus) in his life, he's off on another new obsession, leaving all his newfound possessions to gather dust in the corner.

Have you ever met someone like this? How does he make you feel? The word that comes to my mind is *exasperated*. An unfocused company makes buyers feel the same way. But a focused company provides an unspoken assurance, a peace of mind. Buyers understand what the company is about and can more confidently choose it as a customer. If your company suffers from a lack of focus, try finishing any of the following phrases:

- We focus on . . .
- We specialize in . . .
- A best-fit client for us is one who . . .

Don't suffer from the plague of fuzziness. Know exactly what your company does well and for whom. This focus, in turn, will amply reward your company with satisfied customers and higher levels of word of mouth.

V. THOU SHALT NOT USE GOBBLEDYGOOK PROSE

Too many marketers use words to impress instead of to inform. Rather than writing clearly, they string together as many fancy two-dollar words as they can, trying to create an air of importance. Here's a real-life example of what I like to call gobbledygook prose:

> *[The product] is an agile, lightweight process that can be used to manage and control software and product development using iterative, incremental practices. Wrapping existing engineering practices, including Extreme Programming and RUP, [the product] generates the benefits of agile development with the advantages of a simple implementation.*

What are "iterative, incremental practices"? What are "the benefits of agile development" and why should I care about them? What is RUP? Do you have any idea what this product does? I sure don't. Although the company tries valiantly to explain what this product does, the tone eventually makes the reader feel less smart, maybe even stupid.

One way to prevent this from happening is to run all your marketing copy past someone who knows nothing about your industry. A person like this, without any industry baggage, will view your copy with a critical eye. I'm lucky here because my wife, who is a figure skating coach, is my chief "gobbledygook screen." Often, I ask her to review what I've written and more than I care to admit, she catches me trying to sneak a gobbledygook phrase past her. She'll scribble a comment such as "Huh?" in the margin of the page and I know I've been caught red-handed. To avoid writing gobbledygook prose, regularly show your copy to people like:

- Spouses or significant others
- Advisors
- Peers
- Teachers
- Consultants

Then bite your tongue as you read through their comments. This can be some of the most practical advice you'll receive and you'd do well to heed most of it.

VI. THOU SHALT NOT FORSAKE BENEFITS

Twenty-four-hour hotlines. Overnight delivery. Ten gigabytes of memory. What do these things mean to the red-hot prospect—*nothing!* That's because they're all features. Features provide the prospect with details about the product, but they don't indicate what the prospect gains from the product. Those are benefits, and they're at the heart of a prospect's needs. For example,

- "Save $1,000 over the course of a year."
- "Contact us when it fits into your schedule."
- "Store even the largest files and never worry about available storage."

These are all examples of benefits that powerfully involve the reader in your copy. Each of these has an emotional payoff (saving money, convenience, and eliminating worry) for the reader that makes him or her *feel* better.

If you're unsure how to link features or benefits, try this exercise: First, write down a descriptive phrase for a business (e.g., legal services). Then ask yourself, "When a prospect buys this, what does she really get?" (e.g., fewer headaches, less wasted time, more money from settlements). Then link the two with the phrase "so you get . . ."

Using this example, you'd write the phrase: *"We provide legal services so you get more money from your settlements."*

I once asked a management consultant what his client ended up with, and the consultant's answer surprised me. "Jay," he said, "because I help this company's president meet his tax deadlines, he *gets to participate in the fishing opener.*" If you're a fisherman, you know how important this is.

To spark your thinking on the benefits you offer to others, I've developed two charts (see Figure 2.2) that list the more common benefits, some of which you may be able to borrow:

FIGURE 2.2 *Some Common Benefits*

To a Consumer:		
Wants to gain . . .	**Wants to save . . .**	**Wants to feel . . .**
■ Popularity ■ Advancement ■ Time (vacations, free time)	■ Time ■ Money ■ Embarrassment	■ Happy ■ Loved ■ Whole ■ Valuable
Wants to help . . .	**Wants to be . . .**	**Needs . . .**
■ Others ■ The environment ■ God	■ A recognized authority ■ Up-to-date ■ A good parent	■ Love ■ Respect ■ Laughter ■ New perspectives
To a Business Buyer:		
Develops relationships	**Speed**	**Problem avoidance**
■ Deepen trust ■ Improve credibility ■ Build loyalty	■ Faster decision ■ Faster delivery ■ Faster inventory turns	■ Avoid litigation ■ Battle negative PR spin ■ Risk identification
Increased sales	**Personal satisfaction**	**Fresh perspectives**
■ Increase revenues ■ Increase market share ■ More loyal customers	■ Prestige of working with your company ■ Safe place to talk	■ New learning ■ "No baggage" opinions ■ Unique approaches

"Features tell, benefits sell" is a common saying in marketing and the more you abide by it, the more your copy will attract buyers like a bee to honey.

VII. THOU SHALL COMMIT TO THE RULE OF SEVEN

We marketers could learn a lot about patience from Mother Nature. For example, did you know it takes 10,000 acorns to produce a single oak tree? It takes a cave stalactite 100 years to grow an inch. It takes a coral reef 20 years to grow a foot.

Still not ready to accept patience as a virtue? Just look at these statistics from the National Sales Executive Association that show the percent of online sales that are generated from each point of contact:

- 2 percent on the first contact
- 3 percent on the second contact
- 5 percent on the third contact
- 10 percent on the fourth contact
- 80 percent on fifth to twelfth contacts
  Source: National Sales Executive Association

It's hard to fathom that eight out of every ten online sales are closed somewhere *between the fifth and twelfth contact* between the buyer and the site. Yet, I doubt you'd overhear any of your board members say at the next meeting, "Okay, let's launch this brand-new e-commerce site, and then we'll just sit back and wait for our buyers to make contact with us five times before making a sale."

Let's go back to the oak tree. If it takes 10,000 acorns to produce one oak tree, then that's a response rate of *just .01 percent.* Would your company's leadership be happy with that number? Probably not. Take a page from Mother Nature's handbook and realize that marketing is a numbers game that requires time.

VIII. THOU SHALL AVOID THE WE DISEASE

If you talk too much about your own capabilities, you commit the cardinal sin of the We Disease. Next time you visit a company's Web site, count the number of times it uses the word *we* versus the word *you.* If the Web site is anything like the ones I see, you'll see at least three "we's" for every "you." This is significant because your buyers really don't want to hear about your company. They only want to hear about how your company is going to *help them.*

Too many companies drone on endlessly about a special process they have invented or a certain piece of equipment. Printing companies are especially guilty of the We Disease when they focus too much energy talking about their machines, rather than on what the buyer wants to get from those machines. Printers: Buyers don't care about your presses. Buyers only care that you finish their jobs on time and under budget. Focus on those benefits first, and then you can tell them all about your machines.

To link your company identity with solving your buyers' problems, use the *you* word more often. Here are three examples of you statements that will go a long way towards eliminating the We Disease from your identity:

- Are you still searching for a printer with short-run color capabilities?
- You might wonder how a printer can turn around a job in 24 hours or less.
- Does your printer ever hit the budget number you give them?

To guard against the We Disease, reread any section of new marketing copy and circle all the instances of *we* in red pen. Then go back through the same copy and circle all the instances of the word *you* in black pen. Each word should be used 50 percent of the time.

IX. GIVE THY BUYERS CONTROL WITH OPT OUT

A recent Yankelovich Partners study revealed that 65 percent of respondents feel "constantly bombarded" with too many marketing messages. A full 61 percent felt that the volume of promotional messages is "out of control." Because of this, people are turning to devices that keep the marketers at bay and regulate the flow of promotional messages. These opt-out devices, which put the control back into the buyers' hands, include:

- the mute button on your television,
- the National Do-Not-Call list,
- e-mail spam screening software,
- caller ID,
- pop-up ad blockers, and
- TiVo.

To be sure, these developments make a marketer's job more difficult. But the alternative is to shove a misguided marketing campaign down the throats of unwitting buyers, and run the risk of a buyer backlash. An unfortunate event like this could jeopardize a company's existence. Instead, use opt-out techniques in all your marketing campaigns to reduce this risk.

Always include an opt-out box like the one shown in Figure 2.3 in all your promotional efforts. It will put the control exactly where the buyer expects it these days—in his or her own hands:

FIGURE 2.3 *Opt-Out Option*

OPT OUT?

If you've received this newsletter by mistake or want to be taken off the list,
please e-mail me at *lipe@emergemarketing.com* or call 612-824-4833 and leave a message.

X. THY COMPANY IDENTITY NEEDS CARE AND FEEDING

Nothing in business (or life for that matter) is ever accomplished without working on it daily. Could your company ever get all its accounting work completed if it limited that work to one day a month? Could a manufacturing plant build, package, and ship all its orders one day a month? Could a sales office save up all its sales calls, presentations, and meetings and conduct them every Friday? No way. Each of these company functions requires ongoing, daily effort. Marketing is no different. Companies that are successful marketers, and possess standout company identities, have found a way to work on marketing day in and day out. To them, marketing, like accounting, production, and sales, is an ongoing process that has its own set of care and feeding tasks such as

- auditing touchpoints for quality,
- researching buyers about your identity,
- developing plans to improve your identity,
- implementing improvements to identity materials,
- improving human touchpoints between your market and buyers,
- communicating with outside vendors on identity matters, and
- training internal staff on improvements made to the identity.

Remember, great company identities are made, not born. If you're really serious about improving your company's brand identity, one measure of your company's commitment to this objective will be scheduling time and resources towards its achievement.

CHAPTER WRAP

Sure, from time to time, we may come up short living up to these commandments. But if you consistently break these Ten Commandments of winning company identities, you risk an exodus—a customer exodus.

3

TAKE THE COMPANY
IDENTITY QUIZ

Marketing takes a day to learn, but a lifetime to master.

PHIL KOTLER

THE COMPANY IDENTITY QUIZ

Take this quiz to determine the strength of your company's identity. Just answer the following 20 questions on a scale of 1 to 5, with 5 meaning you totally agree and 1 meaning you don't agree at all. Add up your scores and then find your company's identity score in the table at the end of the quiz.

Totally agree	Somewhat agree	Agree	Somewhat disagree	Totally disagree
5 pts.	4 pts.	3 pts.	2 pts.	1 pt.

1. _____ We have a mission statement that is brief, clear, and inspirational.
2. _____ Every employee in our company has a clear understanding of what a best-fit target customer is for our company.

3. _____ We have a positioning statement that clearly defines our company's point of difference.

4. _____ We use research to gather information about our company identity, and then use the findings to help guide improvements to it.

5. _____ We constantly work to deliver service that is timely, ethical, and focused on meeting the needs of customers.

6. _____ We have clear strategies behind our pricing and we work hard to sell the value built into our prices.

7. _____ We focus our marketing communications around a few, select key messages that are drawn from known customer needs.

8. _____ Our company name is distinctive, memorable, and protected.

9. _____ We have a tagline that further reinforces the company's reason for being and is featured prominently on all our identity materials.

10. _____ We have a distinctive, professional logo that is featured prominently on all our identity materials.

11. _____ We have a standard company color and preferred color schemes that are consistently displayed across all our identity tools.

12. _____ Our business cards, letterhead, and envelopes all use common imagery found in our other visual identity tools.

13. _____ We have a high-quality brochure that reinforces our company identity, makes a compelling case for doing business with us, and then provides concrete next steps for the buyer to take.

14. _____ We have a high-quality Web site that prominently features our company identity, contains valuable information for our buyers, and is easy to navigate.

15. _____ Our company makes a common elevator speech (a short description of what your company does—see Chapter 20) available to all its employees for help in crafting our company identity.

16. _____ We have a clear plan for implementing a company identity program.

17. _____ We insist on consistently displaying all our company identity elements throughout all our marketing vehicles.

18. _____ We use metrics to measure the effectiveness of our overall marketing program, as well as to measure the performance of specific initiatives.

19. _____ Details of our company identity, and the strategies behind it, are well documented and are available to all pertinent internal and external audiences.

20. _____ Everyone in our organization knows what our company identity is and can articulate it clearly

Score Your Company Identity

86–100 points. Congratulations! Your company identity is a superstar. Go to the head of the class.

76–85 points. You have a great start on your company identity, but face a bit more work ahead. Tackle one new identity element this year.

66–75 points. Your company identity is so above average. Identify three new marketing initiatives and get after them.

51–65 points. Can we talk? Your company identity has issues. Commit resources to addressing your five most pressing identity issues.

Under 50 points. Well, you can pack it in or tell yourself it can't get much worse. You have a lot of work ahead of you. Hire a consultant to conduct a full-scale audit and then reassign resources to address your issues—fast.

CHAPTER WRAP

Ralph Waldo Emerson once said that life is a progress and not a station. I hope you'll take that advice to heart as you discover those areas where your company identity needs help and then set about correcting them.

STRATEGIC FACTORS

*The Art of Thinking Through
Your Identity*

4

HOW TO CRAFT A MISSION STATEMENT

See It, Then Say It

Good business leaders create a vision, articulate the vision, passionately own the vision, and relentlessly drive it to completion.

JACK WELCH, Ex-Chairman, General Electric

As an 11-year-old kid, I dreamed of playing shortstop for the Chicago Cubs. In my most vivid daydream, I was in a major-league ballpark, positioned deep at short with a baseball cap pulled down over my eyes, lightly sweeping the dirt back and forth with my right foot.

Fast-forward 35 years to the present: My 11-year-old son, participating in a University of Minnesota Baseball Camp, was invited to scrimmage in the Metrodome—the home of the Minnesota Twins major-league baseball team. After watching his scrimmage for several hours, I turned to leave. As I glanced back at the field one last time, I was startled by what I saw: My 11-year-old kid, in a major-league ballpark, positioned deep at short with a baseball cap pulled down over his eyes, lightly sweeping the dirt back and forth with his right foot.

Folks, never underestimate the power of visioning for your business. Just as clearly as I saw this personal vision come to life, you, too, can see your business vision spring to life. But you must first create, in your mind's eye, a business vision that is so clear, so vivid, and so powerful that it feels like reality. This power of visioning has been explored in depth in such books as *The Magic of Believing* by Claude Bristol, *Think and Grow Rich* by Napoleon Hill, and *The Power of Positive Thinking* by Norman Vincent Peale. If you still question the worth of visioning, read these books. Now, on to the process of crafting your mission statement.

MAKE IT STRAIGHTFORWARD

When I work with a client to develop a marketing plan, I typically interview a number of employees at that company, from a variety of departments and levels within the organization. Sadly, very few of them can remember their company's mission statement. And if I ask to see a copy of the official mission statement, it very often reads something like this:

> *Our mission is to continue to authoritatively coordinate cost-effective services in order to dramatically maintain ethical intellectual capital.*

Huh? You can see, as well as I, that it will be very hard to rally employees around a mumbo jumbo statement like this. Whether the creators of the mission statement had a penchant for using the dictionary, or just had to make the board happy, the end result is a mission statement that won't move any employees to action. Make your mission statement a straightforward statement that is easily understood.

WHAT EXACTLY IS A MISSION STATEMENT?

Definitions of mission statements are as common as graduation parties in June. I like to keep things simple, so here is my definition of a mission statement:

> *A mission statement communicates your company's overriding purpose.*

This definition is purposely broad enough to incorporate elements such as the kinds of business you want to pursue, the target audiences you'll serve, and the contribution your company will make to society. Mission statements are as varied as the companies behind them, but the aim of a mission statement should be the same for every company using one: it should inform everyone who sees it, in no uncertain terms, what the overriding purpose of your business is.

THE THREE CRITERIA FOR A STANDOUT MISSION STATEMENT

I once worked for a company in the home-furnishings industry that was known as a bit of a sweatshop. People routinely worked 14- to 16-hour days and it wasn't uncommon to see fellow employees in the office on both weekend days. In fact, this place was grueling enough that two executives collapsed from the stress—one of them twice. So what was the last bullet point in this company's mission statement?

We will have fun.

Yeah, right. I was so busy working my tail off (and avoiding a collapse myself) that I *never* remember having fun. I recall the first time several of us read this new company mission statement. We laughed out loud, it was so ludicrous. It was at that moment that I learned my most valuable lesson about any mission statement: It has to be real. Otherwise, employees, customers, prospects, investors, suppliers, and even the media will see it as a device that deceives rather than inspires. If you want a mission statement that drives your company forward, keep it real.

Brevity

Someone once asked management guru Peter Drucker how long a mission statement should be. His answer was that it should fit on a T-shirt. Now that's good advice. In today's cluttered environment, tight is right. A short mission statement will not only be easier for your audience to remember, but it will also be easier for your leadership to communicate. The best mission statements run less than 25 words and the really good ones can be summed up in 10 words or less.

Crystal Clarity

If you need a good laugh someday, visit Dilbert's mission statement generator located at *www.dilbert.com* (click on "Games" when you get to the site). Using this tool, you can generate a meaningless mission statement that's created with a random group of verbs, nouns, and prepositional phrases. Among the mission statements it generated for me were:

Our challenge is to authoritatively enhance virtual services while continuing to inter-actively create innovative products to stay competitive in tomorrow's world.

and

We strive to continually supply effective sources so that we may endeavor to interactively foster inexpensive paradigms to set us apart from the competition.

Although the site offers a tongue-in-cheek view of mission statements, the lesson is clear: Far too many mission statements end up being a combination of meaningless phrases and two-dollar words. If you really want to create a mission statement that informs and inspires, make it crystal clear.

Inspiring

Many company leaders tell me the hardest part of their job is keeping employees inspired. The smart ones view a mission statement as a tool that can help them accomplish this. Steve McFarland, CEO of ORBIT Systems, Inc. *(www.orbit.net)*, particularly does a great job of this. His company acts as a virtual IT department for small and midsize businesses, and Steve and his team have grown ORBIT Systems to more than 45 employees and $7 million in revenues. When I first met Steve, I was interviewing him as a finalist for the Twin West Chamber of Commerce's Entrepreneur of the Year award (which he eventually won). During that meeting, he passed out copies of his mission statement and asked us to read it. When I did, my eyes widened. Here is the ORBIT Systems mission statement:

We will be the best customer service organization in the world.

After reading it that day, I wondered out loud if it wasn't a bit over the top. "No, but a lot of our employees wondered the same thing," Steve answered. "Yet you and I know of restaurants with world-famous reputations that people travel the world over to experience. I believe ORBIT can build a similar reputation, right here in our own backyard."

He continued, "I also think that too many companies have forgotten what great customer service is. When was the last time you were in a restaurant or dropped off your car for service and thought to yourself, Wow, that was a *great* experience? It just doesn't happen anymore. When I developed our mission statement I believed then, as I believe now, that we can be the company to set the bar. We will redefine what great customer service is, we will set the bar, and we will be the ones to push it higher every chance we get."

As you can see, Steve grasps a fundamental truth of mission statements: a good one can be written so that it excites and motivates every single employee in your company. I only hope your mission statement will inspire like Steve McFarland's does.

My All Time Favorite Mission Statements

Ford will democratize the automobile.
Ford Motor Company (early 1900s)

To solve unsolved problems innovatively.
3M

To defend the United States through control and exploitation of air and space.
U.S. Air Force

To give unlimited opportunity to women.
Mary Kay Cosmetics

To honor God in all we do. To help people develop. To pursue excellence. To grow profitably.
ServiceMaster Corporation

Dedication to the highest quality of customer service delivered with a sense of warmth, friendliness, individual pride and company spirit.
Southwest Airlines

To make people happy.
Walt Disney Company

To give ordinary folk the chance to buy the same thing as rich people.
Wal-Mart

To boldly go where no man has gone before.
Star Trek

I do one thing. I do it very well. Then, I move on.
Charles Emerson Winchester III (from *M.A.S.H.*)

HOW TO DEVELOP YOUR MISSION STATEMENT

After assembling all the key players in your company, the first step in developing a mission statement is to agree on the criteria you will use to judge its success. At the very least, include the three I've mentioned: brevity, clarity, and inspiration. Other criteria for a successful mission statement are that it:

- defines what we do,
- provides direction for doing the right things,
- addresses our opportunities,
- matches our core competencies,
- is sufficiently broad, and
- reflects the company's values.

After agreeing on these criteria, you're now ready to tackle drafting a mission statement. One good way to begin the discussions is to ask everyone to answer these key questions:

- What business are we in?
- What do we want to be known for five years from now?
- What legacy do we want this company to leave?
- What markets do we want to dominate?
- What position do we want to occupy? Do we want to be number 1? A leader? One of the leaders? A pioneer? A player?
- How far do we want to cover geographically?

At this stage you can expect some lively debate. But gradually, over time, you'll reach a consensus on certain phrases that accurately describe your company's mission. Try to compile as many of these phrases as you can into a one- or two-sentence statement. Here are two examples to show how a short, yet succinct mission statement can be written. Look for the criteria each company has chosen to emphasize in its mission statement:

> *Emerge Marketing will be a leading marketing firm that brings focus to a company's marketing efforts.*

> *Solid Foundations Masonry will be the driving force in the international pre-formed concrete market.*

As you start to craft mission statement options, go for bold and memorable. Sometimes, the bolder a statement is, the more it can actually stretch a company to grow.

It may take three or more drafts to get your mission statement to read correctly. That's OK, for this is the future direction of your company, so take your time. When you finally have a mission statement draft that's close to final, show it to others not in your company. I'm always amazed at the value of an outside perspective. Without company baggage, these folks can give you an honest and unvarnished opinion of your mission statement.

LIPE'S LAW OF MISSION STATEMENTS

If the president of your company can't recite its mission statement, word for word, go back to the drawing board. It's too long or lacks clarity.

PROVEN WAYS TO SPREAD A MISSION STATEMENT FAR AND WIDE

As I'm sure you can imagine, creating your company's mission statement is just the first step. For any mission statement to be an effective company identity tool, you have to consciously communicate it to your employees. How do you do this? Here are a few ideas:

- *Host an event to launch your mission statement.* Make a big deal out of this new (or newly revised) mission statement by hosting a party where you announce it to your employees. The bigger the deal you make out of it, the more attention it will be paid.
- *Make it a desktop item.* Because all marketing benefits from repeated impressions, what about ordering paperweights that contain the mission statement for employees to place on their desks? A gift to your employees like this will be treated with more respect than just another memo from the corner office.
- *Feature it on your intranet.* For larger companies, intranets draw heavy internal traffic and so can be a great place to raise awareness for your mission statement.
- *Make it a permanent feature of internal communications.* Put it in a sidebar that appears in every issue of your internal newsletter. Include it on routing slips or folders. Place a copy by the watercooler. Post it on every company bulletin board. Never pass up an opportunity to promote it internally.

REFER TO THE MISSION STATEMENT OFTEN

The one leader I've seen most effectively communicate a mission statement was our pastor, believe it or not. This gentleman managed to incorporate the church's mission statement into his sermon at least once a month. He would tie it into his sermon theme or just mention it as a reminder ("Let me remind you all of the mission of this church . . ."). And as he would mention the mission statement, it would appear on the overhead screen, for all to read. I must confess I don't go to that church anymore, but I can still recite its mission statement, almost word for word.

Devote time in speeches and presentations to reiterate your company's mission statement. The more you refer to your company's mission statement, the more it will seep into your company identity, and that's good marketing.

SHOULD YOU GO PUBLIC WITH YOUR MISSION STATEMENT?

In my opinion, a mission statement is an *internal* marketing tool only. Its primary use is to direct the actions of employees—not buyers. That's why I advocate not including your mission statement in your company identity materials.

Companies appear pretentious by making a big deal out of their mission statements, while their buyers quietly ask themselves, "Who cares?" Instead, focus your time and energy on internally promoting this mission statement so your employees are clear about what your company stands for. Then trust these employees to internalize the mission statement's key points, and reflect them through their actions.

CHAPTER WRAP

Although primarily an internal marketing device, a mission statement sets the proper direction for all your other company identity programs. Spend a good deal of thoughtful time developing a mission statement that is brief, crystal clear, and inspiring. Then commit equal amounts of time repeatedly communicating it to all those people who can help you achieve its vision.

5

CREATING LASER-LIKE FOCUS ON YOUR TARGET MARKETS

He that is everywhere is nowhere.

THOMAS FULLER, 17th century historian, scholar, and author

If you asked me to identify *the* most important decision in a marketing effort, I'd say it's which audiences your company targets. Think about it. Even if your company were blessed with a breakthrough product, an award-winning brochure and Web site, and a super sales team, none of these would guarantee success. All your efforts would fall on deaf ears if you were talking to the wrong audience.

Let me give you a quick example of a misdirected campaign and how it actually works against marketing success. I've been happily married for more than 20 years, yet I still receive direct-mail solicitations for a dating service. Although I've contacted the company and asked to be removed from its list, I keep receiving its mailings. Do you think, after years of receiving these misguided mailings, that I would ever want to recommend this company to a single friend of mine?

Because this company's effort is so poorly targeted, it annoys me to no end and actually short-circuits any goodwill it could create with me. In the end, this company's identity suffers, at least in my mind.

Correct targeting, however, is a horse of a different color. If you've clearly identified your audience, the pain it feels, and the *solutions* it seeks, your marketing efforts will be like a beacon on a dark winter's night. People (the *right* people) will be naturally drawn to your company.

THE PROSPECTING FUNNEL

For thousands of years, the fundamental process of sales has stayed the same: suspects become prospects and prospects become customers. Shown graphically in the prospecting funnel in Figure 5.1, this time-tested sequence has governed the way companies have marketed themselves for thousands of years, and how they probably will for thousands more.

According to this prospecting funnel, a marketer's first priority is to identify the pool of all *suspects* who need your company's product but haven't yet identified themselves. After these suspects have been identified and marketed to, eventually, some of them will step up to request more information. At this point, they turn into *prospects,* with a qualified need for what your company offers. As a result, the nature of your company's communications must become more personalized to the needs of these prospects. Eventually, prospects learn enough about your company

FIGURE 5.1 *Prospecting Funnel*

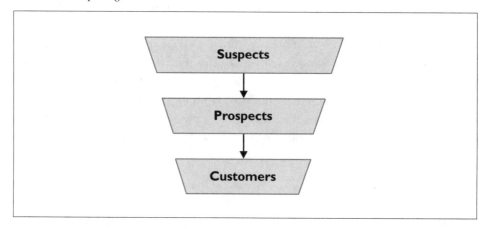

and become comfortable with the idea of purchasing your product. When they purchase, prospects turn into *customers*. At this point, your company's marketing tactics and tenor must change again to ensure that customers remain satisfied, and eventually become ambassadors for your company, spreading positive word of mouth and generating referrals.

When attendees of my seminars first see this prospecting funnel, they naturally ask, "How much time should we spend marketing to each of these three groups?" The answer can be found in my targeting bull's-eye in Figure 5.2.

I recommend that your company spend most of its time and dollars marketing to current customers, because these individuals, well versed in your company's solutions and identity, can offer a rich vein of referrals and word of mouth. If your company nurtures these relationships and subtly asks for their assistance, these customers actually end up acting like an unpaid sales force for your company, and begin spreading the word about your products, services, and company.

While you are marketing to your current customers, you should also be actively marketing to your prospects. The important thing to note is that prospects are in different stages of making a buying decision. Because they have contacted your company to request more information, they have signaled a willingness to establish

FIGURE 5.2 *Targeting Bull's-Eye*

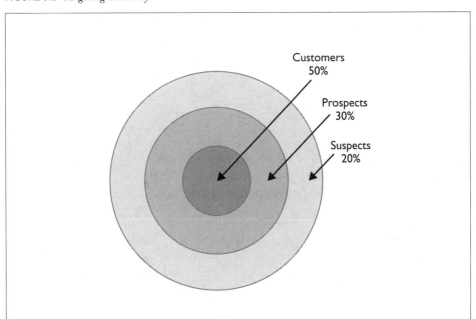

a relationship with your company. Some might have signed up at your Web site to receive e-mails, others might have requested a business card, some could have dropped a card in a trade show bowl, or taken part in any number of other activities. The point is that these prospects have qualified themselves as being more interested than suspects and so should receive a significant portion of your marketing attention.

Marketing to suspects, also called lead generation, brings up the rear, requiring just 20 percent of your time and resources. I know this runs counter to what you hear in the media these days, but lead-generation efforts to cold suspects (those who have no knowledge of your company) will produce prospects that arrive at your company's doorstep without the benefit of a referral or any word of mouth. As a result, building trust and credibility with this class of prospects will require more time (in some cases, years). Effort will have to be spent educating them and making them comfortable with the prospect of doing business with you. I'm *not* saying forsake all lead-generation efforts. I *am* saying pursue lead-generation efforts only after you have a solid customer and prospect marketing effort in place, and pursue it in the right proportion.

In marketing I've seen only one strategy that can't miss–and that is to market to your best customers first, your best prospects second and the rest of the world last.

JOHN ROMERO

LIPE'S LAW OF TARGETING

Some companies I consult with suffer from having *too many* target audiences. This may sound like an enviable problem to have, but it ultimately ends up diluting a company's resources and attention. To help these companies prioritize their target audiences, I use a model that incorporates the following criteria:

- The size of each target audience
- The strength of their need for your product or service
- The available dollars each target group has to spend on a product like yours
- The ability to market to each target audience

If you need to prioritize your target audiences, pick a few of these criteria and then grade each audience using a 1 to 5 scale for each (5 = strong, 1 = weak). After grading all your audiences, identify the top two or three and focus exclusively on them.

SIX REASONS WHY TARGETING CUSTOMERS IS A SMART DECISION

Don't underestimate the importance of marketing to current customers. Here are the top reasons why marketing to existing customers should be your number one priority:

1. *Satisfied customers act as your unpaid sales force.* What's the most powerful marketing tool out there? Positive word of mouth. Happy customers talk about your company and this word of mouth creates awareness, credibility, and new customers. In the end, this word-of-mouth advertising will cost your company far less than other, more traditional forms of advertising.

2. *They already understand your company identity.* You don't need to spend valuable time and money educating satisfied customers about your company brand. Over time, they know what your company stands for and have already established its image in their mind.

3. *Repeat business costs less and is more profitable.* According to statistics from the Boston Consulting Group, it costs *five times less* to generate a sale from a current customer than from a brand-new customer. And because repeat orders involve lower administrative and marketing costs, these sales are more profitable.

4. *Current customers provide honest, immediate feedback.* If, for any reason, your company slips up, you're sure to hear about it from your customers. They'll tell you what they don't like, in no uncertain terms. Don't view these comments as complaints, but rather as valuable opportunities to improve your company.

5. *Customer reorders take less time to process and collect.* Because current customers are already set up in your company's systems, it takes less administrative time to process a repeat order. Plus, repeat customers have an established receivables history with you so you'll know if they're going to pay.

6. *Your customers will feel appreciated.* Sixty-eight percent of all customers stop buying services, or fail to return to a company, if they feel unappreciated, according to the Zeromillion.com Web site. This is the number one reason businesses lose customers.

PROVEN CUSTOMER MARKETING TOOLS

What are some effective ways to market to existing customers? Here are just a few:

- *Ongoing research.* Because frequent customers know your business better than almost anyone else, their feedback can be a treasure trove. In addition, just about everybody likes to be asked for their opinion. The sheer act of listening to your customers' feedback will elevate the relationship even further.
- *Thank them often.* Sadly, we live in an age of bad manners. Most people intend to thank others, but few follow through. Someone in your company should be responsible for writing and sending thank-you notes to customers for recent purchases, providing testimonials, or giving referrals. I can almost guarantee that sending thank-you notes will make your company stand out from the crowd. Plus, it's a warm gesture in today's increasingly frosty world.
- *Customer-appreciation incentives.* Offer your regular customers special, value-added items that others don't receive. These could be white papers, premiums, complimentary items, or a loyalty card good for special offers and discounts.
- *Send reminders for regularly scheduled service.* Lawn-care companies send lawn-treatment reminders in the late winter, hair salons mail reminders six weeks after a haircut, and dry cleaners send out notices to have winter clothes cleaned and stored for the spring. By anticipating a future need for your customers, you'll provide a valuable service—and your company will be remembered for it.
- *Advance sale notices.* Send all your customers an invitation to shop for sale items a few days before the sale is officially announced. This makes customers feel as if they're receiving a "special treatment," and they are.

HOW TO PROFILE YOUR TARGET MARKETS

If you own a tanning salon, a Web-based collectibles company, or a coin-operated Laundromat, your primary buyers are *consumers*. In *business-to-consumer* (B2C) businesses like these, you can use my PAL approach to help target your audience. This acronym helps you remember the three most effective ways to identify your consumers. They are:

- **P**rofile
- **A**ffinity
- **L**ocation

Profile

Your target's profile establishes the *demographics* of your audience. Demographics are statistics about the socioeconomic makeup of your audience and include:

- Age
- Gender
- Marital status
- Household size
- Presence of children
- Ages of children
- Ethnic group

- Education
- Occupation
- Religion
- Principal language spoken
- Home ownership
- Type of car owned

Using two or three of these categories, see if you can define your audience in a single sentence. This could be as simple as saying your audience is *"Married, stay-at-home moms with preschool children"* or *"Spanish-speaking males, age 35 to 54 with full-time jobs."*

Affinity

Once you've established a better profile of your audience, try to uncover the significant relationships in their lives. These *affinities* might include:

- Grade schools and high schools attended
- Colleges attended
- Advanced-degree programs
- Church affiliation
- Fraternal organizations (e.g., Kiwanis)
- Service organizations (e.g., VFW)
- Fraternities/sororities
- Clubs
- Community groups
- Recreational teams
- Internet service providers
- Employers

For example, if you talk to me as a white male in his 40s, then I listen with one ear. But if you talk to me as a member of the Sigma Phi Epsilon fraternity, of which I'm a member, you now have my full attention.

Location

One other effective way to target, especially for smaller businesses, is geographically. Depending on your business's ability to deliver its products and services, your targeting location could be as small as a three-block radius or as large as the entire world.

Here are some common ways of targeting geographically:

- By city block
- Postal carrier route
- Neighborhood
- Zip code
- City
- Metropolitan Statistical Area (MSA)
- State
- Country

WHAT IF YOU SELL TO BUSINESSES?

If you sell to other businesses, yours is a business-to-business (B2B) company and you'll target audiences in a different fashion altogether. Here your targeting takes on two different dimensions. You'll not only research and profile the *businesses* you're targeting (e.g., Midwestern wood manufacturers), but you'll also profile the *people* within these businesses who purchase your product. So, the first three questions you'll have in the B2B targeting process are:

1. What *types* of businesses buy from a company like yours?
2. Who are the *decision makers* within these companies?
3. Who are the *gatekeepers* to a purchase decision?

Profiling Your Target Businesses

When I ask business owners "What kinds of businesses do you sell to?" I very often get the answer "All kinds"—and that's perfectly normal. But when I follow up that question with "Which of these businesses are the *best fit* for your product?" I'm greeted with blank stares. You see, many companies chase after every single prospect, and to be perfectly honest, I made the same mistake when I started my business. I actively pursued Fortune 500 businesses, midsize businesses, and even single-person, freelance businesses. It didn't matter to me as long as they paid on time.

After a while, though, my clients got confused, and had trouble referring business to me. More and more I found them asking me, "Which businesses are the best fit for *your* service?"

If you sell to businesses, use one or all of these three methods to target:

1. Vertical or horizontal marketing
2. Company size
3. Geography

Vertical marketing defined. Instead of choosing to market to everybody (always a losing proposition in marketing), you could decide to vertically market your company, focusing on distinguishable industries, or vertical markets. For example, a wood components manufacturer might concentrate on the following vertical markets: cabinet shops, furniture makers, and point-of-purchase display manufacturers.

Another example of a company that vertically markets is a company that develops herpetology software (software that catalogs the eating and mating habits of snakes and lizards). This kind of company might focus on the following vertical markets: pet stores, zoos, and state parks. The benefits to using a vertical market approach are:

- It's easier to establish your company as the expert in a vertical market. Because you have proven experience with a more specific market segment, your reputation (assuming your products and services are on target) will spread quicker throughout the segment.
- Because you've identified a smaller niche within the overall market, the costs of communicating and promoting your business may be less.
- Your internal staff can become more focused on the needs of this vertical audience. Employee expertise may not have to span as much; however, be aware that prospects in these vertical segments will come to expect expertise from your organization. Be prepared to deliver it.

Horizontal marketing. When a company horizontally markets itself, it concentrates on a target segment that can be found across all industries. For example, a client of mine supplies Add/Move/Change telecommunications services to Fortune 500 companies. This company typically calls on IT department heads. In this horizontal market (IT department heads at Fortune 500 companies), my client doesn't really care if the prospect manufactures cereal, provides tax services, or distributes musical instruments. As long as the target satisfies the conditions of size (Fortune 500) and job function (IT department head), it's a prospect.

The benefits to marketing in a horizontal fashion are:

- There are a greater number of suspects to target in a horizontal market.
- Your product (or service) line doesn't have to be so broad. If you have the right product for a horizontal audience, you can make more sales from it without running out of qualified prospects.
- Word of mouth is likely to be greater for your business because, unlike a vertical market, your horizontal audiences probably don't view your other prospects as competitors.

Using company size to target. You can also target certain businesses by their size using either company revenues or employee count as the yardstick. Let's say your company offers outsourced human resources to other companies. You may determine that companies with revenues in the range of $1 million to $20 million are a best fit because companies that size face human resource issues, yet can't afford to hire a full-time HR staff member. Knowing this revenue range will help you better qualify prospects as you talk with them.

Another way to qualify target companies on size is by employee count. Imagine you sell a product to home-based businesses. You know these companies are largely one-person companies operating out of their homes. If, for instance, you're buying a mailing list of leads to send a postcard to, you can narrow your list criteria to just those companies that show employee counts of one.

Targeting businesses by geography. You may also choose to target your customers geographically. The real advantage to this approach is focus. By selecting geographic boundaries, you will force your company to focus on perfecting its reputation and identity within a given geography. You'll also find that specifically defining your market in terms of a local, regional, national, or international market will also improve the focus of your company's order-taking, servicing, distribution, warehousing, and promotional efforts.

Who Are the Decision Makers?

If your company sells to businesses, you mistakenly think that profiling those *businesses* is all you need to do. But you also want to profile the *people* you'll be selling to within those businesses. Start by asking yourself who within a company typically approves purchases of your product. Is it the purchasing manager? VP of Marketing? CEO? Chief Financial Officer? Director? Manager? Analyst? Several of these?

When you research this question, you may be surprised at what you find. One client of mine, for example, manufactures thermoformed-plastic packaging shells. The company initially thought purchasing managers were its target. After conducting some basic research, we found that *product designers* were the true decision makers for its packaging. It turned out that my client really excelled at engineering package designs that solved problems (e.g., the high incidence of stolen prepaid calling cards at retail). Once my client could demonstrate its package engineering flair to the product designer, the designers were sold on doing business with the client. All my client then had to do was arrange for the product designers to lobby the purchasing department to hire my client.

Back when I sold mainframe software packages, I learned that the people who carried the real sway for purchasing this product were the *users* of the computer software—data-entry clerks, accounting supervisors, and accountants. Day in and day out they would use the software, so it played a very important role in their daily job duties. If the users didn't like my software, the purchasing department wouldn't ask me back. From this experience, for a product like this, I learned that most of my selling efforts had to be targeted to end users, rather than to purchasing departments.

To determine who to target within a company, answer these questions:

1. Which department(s) and job titles will actually use the product (or service) you provide?
2. Whose job performances are directly affected by your product's performance?
3. Is there a committee that must approve purchases of your product or service? If so, who sits on that committee?

After you've identified the people to target, prioritize them according to who has the influence to make a purchase decision involving your product. From there, you'll begin to formulate your selling strategy. This could be as simple as "Meet with the users first, then talk to purchasing, and after that present to the committee." A little research into the buying habits within your target companies will go a long way towards closing sales later on in your marketing effort.

Don't Forget the Gatekeepers

When I marketed a children's cereal brand, I learned all about *gatekeepers*. As part of our marketing research efforts, I would go into grocery stores and observe families shopping in the cereal aisle. I'd watch a young child pick up a box of cereal, perhaps recognizing the product mascot from a Saturday morning television commercial. Then the child would drag it over to her mother for approval.

Sometimes the mother, examining the nutritional label, would shake her head and say, "No, honey, I don't think we can get this one. How about this one instead?" and reach for another. Other times, the mother would smile lovingly back at the child and put the box in the shopping cart. I didn't realize it at the time, but this was my first experience with gatekeepers.

The mother, as you've guessed by now, was the gatekeeper for this purchase. Without her approval, the customer (the child) couldn't get our product. In business-to-business transactions, a gatekeeper acts in much the same way, wielding considerable influence over the purchase decision, while not actually using the product. You'll find gatekeepers throughout all marketing and selling efforts. The Chief Financial Officer might be the gatekeeper for a company-wide software purchase because, in many companies, the purchasing function reports to the CFO. A CEO might be the gatekeeper for a large-scale machinery purchase because the impact of purchasing this machine will be felt across many departments including production, marketing, finance, purchasing, customer service, and shipping. The Vice President of Marketing could be a gatekeeper when hiring a graphic design firm.

After you learn who the gatekeepers are for your products, then determine exactly what it is they look for in a product like yours. Many times, you'll find it's something quite different from what the consumers of the product look for. The best way to identify these gatekeepers is to ask the question, very early on in the selling process, of everyone you call on, "Which people in your company will be involved in the decision to buy our product?" Keep a running list of these names and you'll start to identify both the purchasers and the gatekeepers.

DEVELOP A TARGET PROFILE

After you gather all this information on your target, try to distill it to a pithy 30-words-or-less profile, such as:

Our target is:
CEOs of U.S. companies with sales between $1 and $50 million
and employee counts between 10 and 100.
Or

Stay-at-home moms in the United States who are stressed for time.

NOW PAINT A PICTURE

One day in a graduate school marketing class, our professor asked us to describe what the male consumer of a Seagram's Wine Cooler looked like. The class then painted a picture of a young, clean-shaven, urban professional who wore a three-piece suit, wingtips, and a conservative tie.

Then the professor asked us to describe the consumer for a Bartles & Jaymes Wine Cooler. This time, we painted a picture of an unshaven surfer dude wearing a floral shirt, shorts, and sandals. This exercise was mind-expanding because even though both guys were white male 20somethings, their lifestyles were as different as night and day.

That's why your targeting effort isn't really complete until you develop a *mind's-eye picture* of your target. This is a written description that captures the lifestyle, thoughts, and emotions of your target audience. Ask yourself these questions:

- What do our buyers look like? How do they dress?
- What kind of cars do they drive?
- What kind of friends do they hang out with?
- How do they feel about life? Are they happy? Sad? Stressed?
- What would be different about their lives if they had our product?

Using this information, write a ministory that describes in vivid detail who this person is and why. This is called a *mind's-eye picture*. Here's an example of one I developed for a travel industry client. It describes a working mom and the pain she feels when planning a vacation:

> *Today's world is different. I'm under constant pressure—time pressures, financial pressures, and the pressure to balance work and family.*
>
> *Funny how planning a vacation just adds more pressure to my life. I have to research all the options and follow up on all the details. It's all up to me to find the right things to do on a limited budget. And even then, the pressure's <u>still</u> on because my husband may not like what I've planned.*
>
> *With one phone call, I want to talk to a knowledgeable travel agent who'll save me time and money and take care of all the details.*

This exercise will hone your empathy skills because you'll be forced to understand how your target *feels* emotionally. Many purchases are based on emotions, so the better you can understand the emotional states your buyers are in, the more your messages will speak directly to them.

KNOW WHO'S IN THE MIDDLE

Let's suppose for a moment that you manufacture a product. You then sell it to a distributor who, in turn, sells it to retail stores, where the customer eventually buys it. The distributor and retailers in this scenario are called *intermediaries*. They're partners in the warehousing, distribution, and promotion of your product, and, as a result, are the first customers for your product. If they don't like your product, you don't stand a chance of getting your product into the hands of the end consumer.

If your business requires intermediaries, it goes without saying that you'll have to identify and profile them, too. To help you do so, rough out a PAL analysis (described previously) for each.

The most commonly found intermediaries are:

- Distributors
- Wholesalers
- Retailers
- Brokers
- Manufacturer representatives
- Dealers
- Value-added resellers

DON'T MISTAKE WELL-TARGETED PROGRAMS WITH CONVENIENT ONES

I once worked with a real estate development firm to market a new development of luxury townhomes located in our downtown area. As it turned out, the head of this firm also owned several fast-food restaurants. His question to me was, "Shouldn't we advertise the property at these fast-food restaurants?" My return question to him was, "Does the target audience for these luxury townhomes eat at these restaurants?" My question took him by surprise.

He saw lots of traffic streaming through his restaurants and automatically assumed that it would translate into qualified leads. I, on the other hand, saw money and someone's precious time being sunk into a program that would market the development to a host of unqualified leads. When was the last time you saw an upper-income person eating at an inner-city fast-food restaurant?

Just because a marketing program is *convenient* doesn't mean it's well targeted. In my opinion, the first question a marketer should ask about any proposed marketing vehicle is, "Will our target audience be there to see our messages?"

CHAPTER WRAP

Spend a lot of time profiling your buyers. This is one of the most important tasks you'll ever do as a marketer. Clear, concise thinking about who wants your product and what motivates them to buy it is of paramount importance to your business. Don't cut corners here.

6

THE BASICS ON POSITIONING YOUR COMPANY SO IT STANDS OUT

Make no mistake about it, the mind is the battleground.

AL RIES, Positioning Guru

Which is faster: a greyhound or an ostrich? Many of you may have answered the greyhound because you had images of this speedy animal racing around a dog track, chasing a funny-looking mechanical bunny. Believe it or not, the ostrich is faster. This flightless bird can reach speeds of 45 miles an hour, and maintain that speed for up to 30 minutes at a time. The greyhound's top speed is a comparatively slow-footed 39 mph.

Wrapped up in this example is the power of positioning. Many of us have *positioned* the greyhound in our minds as a fleet-footed animal even though the ostrich is the faster animal. Perhaps you've positioned the ostrich in your mind as the funniest-looking bird, or maybe the bird that buries its head in the ground. But fast? Never. The lesson here is that we humans position things in our minds—animals, products, and companies—based on the images we are repeatedly exposed to. So if you want your company to be successfully positioned in your buyers' minds, you have to find a position that fits and then hammer this position home to your audience.

WHAT IS POSITIONING?

The real heart of positioning is finding that quality, that dimension, that sets your company apart from all others. To arrive at this quality, first determine

1. what makes each of your competitors unique,
2. what makes your own company unique, and
3. what perceptions your buyers already have of your company and others.

This involves a lot of hard work, but is it rewarding. In fact, if done correctly, positioning lies at the heart of winning the marketing game.

The man who invented the modern art of positioning is Al Ries, coauthor (with Jack Trout) of the book *Positioning: The Battle for Your Mind.* If you read one book about positioning, this should be it. You'll learn all the basics of the powerful art of positioning your company as well as the ironclad rules that Ries and Trout believe you must follow to successfully position your company so it stands out from the crowd.

THE RULES OF POSITIONING

The basic rules of positioning as put forth by Ries and Trout are:

Most competition can't be beaten head-on. Let's say your company is a mid-size building contractor and your closest competitor is ten times your size. Let's also say that this supersize competitor has staked out the position of "lowest price." How should you position your company?

You can't successfully position your company as "lowest price," because your competitor has successfully staked out this position already. A better move might be to stake out, for example, the "high-touch service" position. If your company can deliver on this promise (e.g., weekly face-to-face project meetings with all clients, monthly phone calls from your president to the president of each client, and a pass-word-protected Web site enabling clients to access up-to-the-minute project plans), then you'll attract the segment of buyers that values this, and end up standing out from the crowd.

Don't waste valuable time and money trying to dislodge your competitor from its existing position. The slot is already filled in your buyer's mind. Instead, a better move is to position your company in a slot that hasn't been filled yet.

Positioning involves sacrifice. For your company's positioning to have oomph, it must have focus. And focus, by its very definition, means giving up other benefits with lesser values. You can't be the "lowest price contractor that offers high-touch service." Something's got to give. Stake your claim to one superior benefit and then hammer this home repeatedly.

There is rarely just one position a company can take, but there is always a best one. One client of mine was a $500 million business travel agency that had positioned itself as "the low-fare provider." As part of my marketing planning process, I interviewed five of its biggest customers. During our conversations, I learned that none of these companies saw my client as a low-cost provider. Instead, they saw the client as an expert in providing travel management services (e.g., proactively reporting on travel patterns, consulting on cost-saving changes, and providing outsourced travel functions).

From this, we decided to reposition the agency as a "travel management company." This was a far more accurate (and lucrative) positioning than its "low-fare provider" status. After a major rebranding effort, driven by this repositioning, the company ended up doubling its sales over the next five years.

Good positioning repositions your competitors. The best example of this is the 7UP soft drink and its "Uncola" positioning in the 1970s. Up until that time, Coke and Pepsi owned the top two positions in the cola category. All anybody seemed to drink were colas. So the brains behind 7UP created a new category called the "Uncola." By positioning the drink as an Uncola, 7UP brilliantly lumped all cola drinks together as the same drink and positioned 7UP as uniquely different. Sales of 7UP jumped 10 percent the very first year and, just as important, an alternative category was born. Now anytime anyone says "Uncola," what do you think of?

THREE GOOD REASONS TO POSITION YOUR BUSINESS

1. You will avoid the "muddle in the middle." This amorphous lump of competitors occurs at the midprice range because higher-end products position themselves as "prestige" items, while lower-priced ones assume the "low-price" label.

That leaves everyone else to slug it out in the midprice tier. Because so many companies fall into this "muddle in the middle," the risk of not selecting a position is that your company will blend in with the others. Buyers won't understand what makes your company unique and, as a consequence, your company *will not stand out*.

If your company finds itself in the "muddle in the middle," work hard to find a positioning that distinguishes your company on this dimension. If you do this, you'll find your company identity spreading like mushrooms after a spring rain.

2. Solid positioning helps your company defend its turf. As new competitors enter your market, it will help immensely if you've already staked out a discernible positioning. Buyers will recognize your company as the company that makes the most durable products on the market (*or* takes the most creative approaches to solving client problems *or* is the most environmentally friendly builder, etc.). Defending your turf becomes more of an exercise in supporting your unique position so you remain distinctive from competitors.

3. Strong positioning can reduce your marketing expenditures. Well-positioned companies enjoy a unique awareness among buyers. As a result, they benefit from stronger word of mouth in their market and this, in turn, means you won't have to shout so much. That's a good thing because shouting costs a lot of money these days.

WHY LOW-PRICE POSITIONING IS SUICIDE

One big mistake I see companies of all sizes make is positioning their companies as the low-price provider. Wal-Mart can do this ("Everyday low prices"), but my guess is you can't. You'd need an army of arm-twisting purchasing agents, a state-of-the art distribution system, and a bare-bones staff to pull it off.

Being the low-priced company also shifts the emphasis away from the value your product or service provides. Once your company identity gets tied up with lowball pricing, you face an uphill battle getting your market to focus on any other marketing dimension (e.g., unique product features or outstanding service). Rolling out a new product with a host of bells and whistles will be greeted with just one question from your buyers: "What's the best price I can get?"

When you position your company on low price, you also limit your ability to raise prices in the future. It's an undeniable fact that your company's costs, over time, will rise. After exhausting all cost-reduction options, you'll be forced to raise your prices. But if your company has staked its identity on a low-price position, your price increases will be met with scorn. Buyers will perceive your price increase as out of sync with your positioning, and your identity will suffer from a lack of consistency.

Stay away from a low-price positioning. For most companies, it's as wrong as two left shoes.

LIPE'S LAW OF POSITIONING

Use Discounts Sparingly

I was recently approached by a program director about giving a speech titled, "How to Successfully Market Your Self-Published Book" (my first book, *The Marketing Toolkit for Growing Businesses*, was self-published). After numerous back-and-forth conversations about the event, she e-mailed me asking, "We'll be offering 25 percent discounts on our books; would you like to do the same?" I answered back that my policy on discounting products was: "I don't." After she pressed me to explain my reasoning, I answered that discounting lowers a product's perceived value. Instead, I preferred to offer something of added value, like a special report, a white paper, or a checklist.

Discounting subtly communicates to your audience that your list price isn't really your final price. Once buyers perceive this, they'll negotiate harder to find your final price. Instead of discounting, try offering one of these value-added features:

- Unique information (e.g., special reports)
- An added-service component (e.g., a free deodorizing treatment with any car wash)
- Extended service coverage (e.g., an extended warranty)

SOME COMMON WAYS TO POSITION YOUR COMPANY

Here are some of the more valuable ways to position your company. This is not meant to be an exhaustive list, just a place to begin the discussion. Be creative when deciding what your company's unique point of difference is.

- *Widest selection positioning.* If you have the wherewithal to stock many, many items, you can position your company as having the widest selection of products on the market. You'll find this positioning used by superstore retail operations and many e-commerce Web sites.

- *Industry niche positioning.* Becoming a dominant provider in a specific industry is a positioning strategy that many technology firms take. Before the advent of the iPod, Apple Computer focused on the graphic design industry. One clear benefit is that vertical industry expertise like this often commands higher prices.
- *Problem-solving positioning.* Is there a problem your market agonizes over? If so, position your company as the one that has the answer. One enterprising contractor, whose positioning was the "Keep It Clean Contractor," promoted the fact that he owned more ShopVacs then any other contractor in the market.
- *Unserved niche positioning.* Adams Golf recognized that its much larger competitors were battling it out for golfers' attention on the tees (drivers) and the greens (putters). They wisely chose to establish themselves in an uncontested market: fairway woods. After introducing a line of patented fairway woods called the Tight Lies Fairway Woods, they successfully outflanked their much-larger competition.
- *Customer service positioning.* Most everyone knows the story of Nordstrom's over-the-top customer service. Just listen to what the company says about its commitment to service: "We remain committed to the simple idea our company was founded on: earning the trust of our customers, one at a time." Can you deliver a higher standard of service than your competitors? Train your employees to provide remarkable customer service, and word of mouth about your company will flow like champagne at a wedding.
- *The local edge positioning.* If your company enjoys a local presence, and your competitors don't, use this to your advantage. Touting the advantages of your "on-site service" or "warehouse just around the corner" can be powerful differentiators for your company identity.
- *Guarantee positioning.* Can you offer a guarantee so strong no one else in your industry matches it? When I worked for an innovative mattress manufacturer, we offered a 90-Night Sleep Guarantee; if you didn't like the mattress after sleeping on it for 90 nights, you could return the mattress for a full refund. The company even paid the return shipping.
- *Green positioning.* The growth of eco-friendly products has risen markedly. Brands such as the Body Shop and Patagonia are the standard-bearers for this positioning. Companies such as General Mills, Heinz, Kraft, and Kellogg have all jumped on the bandwagon recently by acquiring or purchasing green brands. One Web-hosting company I know of positions itself as the "green Web-hosting company" because it uses 120 solar panels that are mounted on the roof of its data center to power its servers.

- *Integrity positioning.* A client of mine in the commercial building business once said, "Other commercial contractors tell you what you want to hear; we tell you what you need to know." This is solid positioning based on integrity. If you can back up this positioning, it can be extremely effective. But remember, all it takes is one ethical lapse, one white lie, and your position is undermined forever.
- *Distribution positioning.* The way customers obtain your product can also uniquely position your company identity. In its early days, Amazon.com was the clear leader in the online book category. As a result, it created a unique position for itself.
- *Competitive superiority positioning.* Many of you remember the Pepsi Challenge versus Coke taste tests back in the 1970s. If you can position your company around a significant competitive advantage (and, better yet, prove it with quantifiable research), you'll stand out from the crowd.
- *Offer positioning.* Can you become known by an offer you make? I've heard about an accountant that offers his tax preparation clients a 100 percent refund on their preparation fee if they refer four new clients. They are known as the "100 percent refund tax guys."
- *Speed of service positioning.* Most notable here is FedEx's "Absolutely, Positively Overnight" positioning. This positioning is so clear and understandable that it has made its way into our modern-day lexicon. I also know a service provider who claims he "returns all phone calls within 24 hours." This is an intriguing claim, given that it takes many people days, or even weeks, to return my phone calls.

This is just a start. The number of ways to position your company is limited only by your imagination. Now let's move on to how you can arrive at the right positioning for your company.

HOW TO COME UP WITH YOUR COMPANY'S POSITIONING

There are three steps to follow when determining your company's positioning.

1. Identify Your Company's Strengths

Positioning is a concentrated focus on what you do better than every other company does. So the first step is to get a handle on what things you do best as a company. To help you identify this, work with your executive staff to answer to these questions:

- How do we make the lives of our customers better?
- What do we do better than all other competitors do?
- How do we want our company to be remembered?

By all means, you should be asking your clients and customers these same questions on a regular basis.

2. Evaluate Your Competitors

Next, you'll want to evaluate the competitive landscape. Once you know your company's strengths, you should weigh these against your competitors' strengths. Ask several of your customers these questions:

- Which companies do we compete against?
- What do these competitors do better than us?
- What do we do better than them?
- Which companies must be outgunned to achieve this position?

3. Use Brackets

I learned this approach to positioning when I worked in marketing for General Mills. Use the following "brackets" and see if you can complete the sentence for your company:

[Your company's name]
is the

[category where you compete, e.g., accounting firm, marketing agency] that's

[your superior quality].

Following are the product positioning statements for two General Mills cereals that resulted from this exercise. They give you an idea of how powerful this bracketing technique is:

- Whole Grain Total is the only adult cereal that offers 100 percent RDA of 12 essential vitamins, plus iron.
- Fruit Roll-Ups is the real fruit snack that's fun to eat.

You want to end up with a positioning statement that shows off your defining point of difference. If you do, you'll have uncovered a potent marketing weapon.

What's Your Company's Make and Model?

One day in a meeting with a client, I decided to have some fun and asked him what kind of car my company reminded him of. I fully expected him to answer with a well-known brand name. Instead he surprised me by answering "a pace car."

Up until that point, I hadn't fully appreciated that for many of my clients, I help bring their organization up to marketing speed. After that happens, I leave their company in hopes that they can continue the marketing race without me.

This analogy, a clear example of positioning, communicates to potential clients what they get out of a working relationship with me. As a result, I weave the analogy into presentations about my work whenever I can.

SOME TIPS FOR SUCCESSFULLY POSITIONING YOUR COMPANY

Own a Word

If you can boil down the essence of your business to just one word, and own that word in people's minds, you've won the positioning battle. Too often when I bring up this idea with business leaders, I meet resistance. "We're known for a lot of things," they say. "We don't want to be known for just one thing."

Sure you are, but so are Federal Express (overnight) and Volvo (safety), yet each of them has crafted a very successful identity around one word. Here are some other examples of organizations whose identities center around a word (or two):

Cars
- Volvo—safety
- BMW—driving experience
- Mercedes-Benz—prestige
- Porsche—sports cars

Retail and apparel
- Nordstrom—service
- Tommy Bahama—sun and surf

Technology
- Google—search
- OnStar—first-aid stories

Graduate schools
- Northwestern's Kellogg School—marketing
- Wharton—finance
- Harvard—management

Entertainment
- Cirque du Soleil—innovative circus

Given our cluttered world, my advice these days is to say less and have it remembered, rather than say too much and have it forgotten. See if you can't condense your company's positioning to one word, then do everything you can to reinforce that word.

Sync Up Your Positioning and Visual Identity

Once you've established the right positioning for your company, make sure all your visual elements reinforce it. All logos, typestyles, color, and design templates should all support your positioning. For example, if you position your company as prestigious, it just doesn't make sense to use a cute logo.

Try This Authenticity Test

Once you've finished your positioning statement, test its authenticity by swapping your name with your competitor's name. If you can read the same statement with your competitor's name now featured and not bat an eye, you need more work on your positioning statement. Remember, an accurate positioning statement clearly distinguishes your company from every other company.

WHY A POSITIONING STATEMENT SHOULD NEVER SHOW UP ON YOUR WEB SITE

Quite simply, a positioning statement is for internal use only. It should be used to guide internal discussions and direct the work of others, but it is *not* a communications device for the outside world. Taglines, logos, slogans, copy, and just about every other external identity tool will draw from your positioning statement. But your positioning statement should be kept on a need-to-know basis only.

CHAPTER WRAP

Let me close out the chapter with one last animal question: Which is the fastest animal on our planet? Is it the . . .

1. Cheetah?
2. Gazelle?
3. Lion?
4. Antelope?
5. Peregrine falcon?

The fastest animal on earth, *by a factor of almost three,* is the peregrine falcon. During one of its dives (called a *stoop*), a falcon can reach speeds in excess of *185 miles per hour.* Meanwhile the cheetah, gazelle, lion, and antelope bump along at less than 80 miles per hour.

Hard to believe, isn't it? But the question again demonstrates the power of positioning. Because most of us have been exposed to images of cheetahs, gazelles, or antelopes racing across the savanna, we have positioned them as incredibly fast. But a peregrine falcon? Who has ever been exposed to this bird's speed?

Let this be a lesson for your company. To position your company successfully, you must first know what your company excels at, and then work hard to position that quality in your buyers' minds so it is remembered instinctively.

MARKET TOUCHPOINTS

Tools That Create Dialogues

7

THE ART OF LISTENING

Market Research Tools That Any Company Can Use

Somewhere, something incredible is waiting to be known.

CARL SAGAN

For thousands of years, people have been conducting market research. I don't mean with fancy focus groups or complicated conjoint analysis. I mean just by asking questions and listening to the answers. Using this art of listening, as I like to call it, is so crucial, so fundamental to the success of your company identity, that to deny it is to invite failure. Follow along as I show you how to leverage marketing research so it funnels valuable knowledge into your identity-building program.

WHY RESEARCH IS SO IMPORTANT TO COMPANY IDENTITY

Recently I sat on a panel of experts that was advising would-be consultants how to successfully launch a consulting practice. As an exercise, we asked the participants to describe their future consulting practice. Each one in the room took a turn at answering the question. Most folks described their consulting practices in terms of satisfying their desires for intellectual challenge, interaction with other intelligent people, and a decided absence of office politics. To a person, every single one described his or her future consulting practice by explaining how it was going to satisfy *his or her* desires.

I listened patiently and waited for everyone to finish. Then I asked the group, "What kind of consulting work are *your clients* looking for?" You could have heard a pin drop. Not one of these very intelligent people had conducted any research with future clients to determine what *they* might want from a consultant.

That exercise took me back to the days in the early 1990s when I started my own consulting business. As part of my marketing plan, I wrote on a piece of paper a 100-word description of what my consulting practice would look like that included:

- The target audience for the practice,
- What these buyers wanted from a consultant, and
- How my practice would be different from others.

Then I set up coffee appointments with 20 business leaders and put this written description in front of them. After asking for their feedback, I sat back and listened. Their advice was invaluable. I learned that my positioning—focusing on growing companies with a time-starved marketing department—was on target (it remains my positioning today). I also learned that these kinds of clients were less interested in hearing about my Fortune 500 work experience. Instead, they wanted to see in my marketing materials how I had helped other organizations their size.

Because of this research, I believe my company's identity ended up being more focused, targeted, and ultimately successful.

RESEARCH CAN ALSO PERFECT PRODUCTS

A short while ago, I worked with a major company in the lawn-care products industry. We were launching a brand-new zero-turn radius riding mower. New to this market, the company and I wanted to perfect the product's design before launching. To help us gather consumer feedback, we organized a series of focus groups. Up to this point, I had been working with the internal design team and engineers to develop a product prototype. We were supremely confident that we had designed the right product for the market and viewed the research as a mere rubber stamp for the design. However, when we showed the prototype to the focus

group participants, we were shocked by their reaction. Almost every single partici-
pant didn't care for the front-end design. "Flimsy" and "breakable" were two words
that we heard often, and words that clearly didn't support the brand's positioning.

During the next week, we scrambled to redesign the front end and hastily organized a series of one-on-one research interviews with these same participants to get
feedback on the new design. In the end, they loved it and, as of this writing, the product
has been launched successfully and has contributed significant, incremental revenue to
the company. But I shudder to think what might have happened if we had launched the
product in its original design, without this research. I'm convinced the product would
have bombed, costing the company millions of dollars and tarnishing its reputation.

Your company's research may not be nearly this extensive, but remember the
lesson here: research can and should be used throughout the design of any new
product to generate more successful products.

RESEARCH IS A TOOL FOR DEEPENING RELATIONSHIPS

Whatever the size of your company, you'll find that research strengthens the
bonds between your company and its buyers. The bottom line is: people like it
when you ask for their opinion. Not only will they feel they're contributing to your
company's success, but you'll learn more about their perceptions of:

- Your company identity
- Your competitors
- New areas of opportunity for your company (new markets, new products)

Research firm TARP has found that for every person who complains, 26 others
don't. So, if 10 customers have complained recently to your company, another 260
may have held their tongues while turning to your competitors. Properly conducted
research many times acts as a feedback machine designed to root out these people's
thoughts.

OTHER IMPORTANT PAYOFFS OF RESEARCH

- *Research can reestablish dialogues with long-lost customers.* Sometimes a survey is
  all that's needed to reestablish a dialogue between a company and a customer who feels ignored.

- *Research gives people a chance to vent.* Sometimes people just want to air their feelings. This doesn't mean they will abandon you or your company. To the contrary, they may respect you more for giving them the chance.
- *Research can find new growth opportunities right under your nose.* A client of mine in the health care data industry told me a great story about his company's market research. Several years ago, his half-million-dollar company decided to survey its customers. One of the questions it asked was, "What new products would you like to see us offer?" Of the 90 responses it received, an overwhelming number said they would like to see the company offer market share data. The company moved quickly and within less than a year began offering market share data. The result? His business *more than quadrupled* over the next two years.
- *Research can increase awareness of ancillary products.* Good surveys not only collect data but also disseminate information. As long as it is handled tastefully, you can educate consumers about your company's new products or services with a survey.
- *Research can sometimes reactivate dormant customers.* I once helped an industrial services client survey its past customers, ones it hadn't heard from in more than a year. After asking for their feedback on the previous work, we included the following question: *"Do you know of anyone, in your company or outside of it, who could benefit from the services XYZ provides?"* The response was overwhelming. In the end, the survey generated more than $700,000 in sales from both active and dormant accounts. In addition, numerous new leads were generated.

Competitors' Proposals: A Research Gold Mine

If your customers use proposals to evaluate vendors, ask one of them if you can see your competitors' proposals. Only one out of ten will agree, but when that one does say yes, you'll be astounded by what you learn. Competitors' proposals will divulge their positioning, pricing, key messages, product details, and a host of other information. To avoid putting your client in an awkward position, try phrasing your request like this, "I'd certainly understand if you said no, but would you consider letting me see the other proposals you received?" Of course, do this only after you've won the business.

THE BEST LOW-COST MARKET RESEARCH TOOLS

One-on-One Interviews

This is one of my favorite research techniques. In it, you (or better yet, an outside consultant) speak directly with your company's customers, one at a time. Via phone or in person, you walk the respondent through a standard questionnaire. Each respondent is asked the same questions and the interviews are designed to take less than 30 minutes each.

Use some or all of the questions in Figure 7.1 to conduct these interviews.

FIGURE 7.1 *One-on-One Questionnaire*

Background Questions

1. How long have you been a customer of XYZ Company?
2. How did you first learn about XYZ Company?
3. At that time, why did you become a customer of XYZ Company?

Current Purchasing Environment

4. With respect to [your industry] what are the biggest challenges you face?
5. How does XYZ Company help you with these challenges?

Competitive Environment

6. Who are XYZ's biggest competitors that you deal with? What are their strengths and weaknesses?

Your Company's Profile

7. What are XYZ's greatest strengths? Weaknesses?
8. What does XYZ do that no one else in the market does?
9. What would it take for you to stay with XYZ for five years?

Marketing and Sales

10. What other capabilities or services would you like to see XYZ offer?
11. How often do you hear from XYZ?
12. Which methods does it use to keep in touch with you?
13. Which of XYZ's competitors does the best job of marketing? How does it market its company?

Postpurchase Surveys

To keep the lines of communication open between you and your customers, administer a quick customer-satisfaction survey right after delivering your product or service. It will help your company keep tabs on how well you're doing with your customers, and can also head off potential problems. Given everyone's preoccupation with time, I limit my company's survey to one page—a fax-back survey with just five questions—and 90 percent of all surveys are returned.

Here are some questions that can be used in this type of survey:

- What one thing did you like about doing business with us?
- What one thing would you change about our company?
- When you bought our product, what did you really end up with?
- On a scale of 1 to 10, please rate us on the job we did for you.
- What would it take for you to stay with us for five years?

Networking

These days, networking receives a lot of attention as a lead-generation device, but I also see networking as a market-research vehicle. The next time you or someone from your sales organization sets up a networking meeting, identify one piece of research information you'd like to obtain. It could be something about your major competitor (e.g., *What do you know about ABC Company?*) or something about your typical customer behavior (e.g., *What additional services do you see customers in our market needing?*). Gathering vital research information can sometimes be as cheap as a cup of coffee.

Blogs

Blogs are a great way to encourage dialogues with your market. Savvy marketers are now using blogs to

- elicit instant feedback from customers,
- carry on simultaneous conversations with customers and prospects, and
- facilitate the spread of buzz about your company.

Ever since starting my blog *(www.emergemarketing.com/blog)*, I've noticed that it serves as a useful feedback device. I hear from experts far and wide, and dialogues can sometimes break out between them with me as the moderator. If you're interested in starting a blog, visit *www.typepad.com* or *www.blogger.com*.

A Little-Used, Free Research Tactic

Scour the Sunday classifieds section for ads by your competitors. If they're hiring individuals for a particular department or discipline, you can bet they plan on expanding into it.

Customer Clubs

When I was the marketing director at a mattress manufacturer, each quarter we'd host an informal conversation with our customers. We'd invite five to ten customers to our headquarters and conduct a no-holds-barred conversation about our products and marketing. Boy, were they flattered.

Over popcorn and soft drinks, we'd show them new product prototypes or share preliminary ad concepts. We might even show them proofs of new marketing materials we were developing. All this proved extremely valuable in developing our product mix and marketing messages.

Just as important, these customers left the meetings with a renewed feeling of loyalty. We'd cared enough to ask for their input, and most were very appreciative. I'd highly recommend customer clubs as a valuable (and inexpensive) way to gather market feedback.

Mystery Shopping

Used widely by the retail industry, these studies hire an outsider to pose as a shopper at a company's store. Studies like this help your company identify strengths and weaknesses in the following areas:

- Store appearance
- Service quality
- Selling skills of your personnel
- Product selection
- Pricing

To obtain the best results for this type of research, hire an outside firm and be very specific about the kind of feedback you're seeking.

Usability Testing

If your company's Web site plays a significant role in building the company's identity, you may want to consider *usability testing*. Usability testing determines how well users can interact with your company's Web site. In a typical Web usability test, one or two users sit in a room and use the Web site to perform certain tasks, while company marketers watch, listen, videotape, or take notes. For more information on usability testing, visit the Usability Professionals' Association Web site at *www.upassoc.org* or read Steve Krug's excellent book, *Don't Make Me Think: A Common Sense Approach to Web Usability.*

ONE REASON TO USE OUTSIDERS FOR CUSTOMER RESEARCH

If your company can afford it, consider hiring an outsider—either a consultant or a researcher—to conduct much of this research. Many customers are reluctant to share their true opinions for fear of damaging the relationship. I have interviewed countless customers and prospects for my clients and I'm always a little surprised at how open they are with me. Perhaps they feel more comfortable telling an objective third-party person the unvarnished truth.

CHAPTER WRAP

I've spent more than two decades in the marketing field and one thing I know about companies that are successful marketers is that they commit to research as an ongoing marketing strategy. If you're really serious about improving your company's identity, you must have a market research program in place.

LIPE'S LAWS ON MARKET RESEARCH

1. Always thank respondents after a research session. Send flowers or just a thank-you note, but always find a way to recognize the time and effort they've sacrificed for your company.

2. Whenever possible, try to quantify research results. Phrase questions along the line of "On a scale of 1 to 5, how important is it to you that _____?" This produces data that can be quantified and is easier to draw conclusions from.

3. Mix in open-ended questions with any quantifiable data. Sometimes, people have the most wonderful research insights when you give them the latitude to put it into their own words.

4. If your product is widely distributed, keep your eye on consumer feedback sites like e-pinions (www.epinions.com) and Amazon (www.amazon.com). Some of the most valuable insights into your products will come from these sites because consumers are free to air their true feelings, using their own words.

8

THE KEYS TO DELIVERING WORLD-CLASS SERVICE

A brand is a living entity—and it is enriched or undermined cumulatively over time, the product of a thousand small gestures.

MICHAEL EISNER, Former CEO of Disney

Every so often when I'm hired by a company to develop a marketing plan for its business, after conducting my initial assessment, I discover that the lack of a marketing plan isn't the problem. The real problem is the company's poor service. For these companies, spending any money at all on marketing is like pouring fine wine down a sinkhole—a complete waste.

If your company's service leaves a lot to be desired, fix that first. It's the glue that bonds your company to its market. First and foremost, make sure every employee in your company is driven to provide first-rate, top-of-the-line, I'll-get-that-for-you-right-away service. Then, and only then, should you worry about promoting your company.

TOP TEN CUSTOMER SERVICE MISTAKES

Before learning how a company can offer world-class service, it might be help-ful to point out the most common service problems in business today. Fix these and your company's reputation may well be the only marketing program you need:

10. *Not knowing your products (or services) stone-cold.* You are the expert; that's why customers contact you. If you can't answer their questions immedi-ately, promise to find out the answers and get back to them when you've found them.

9. *Not adequately training your staff.* Financial services call centers in the United States that enjoy the highest customer satisfaction levels routinely invest *180 hours* of initial training and seven hours of ongoing training every year for each agent they employ. Does your company take its service training this seriously?

8. *Trying to win an argument with a customer.* Arguing with a customer is bad business. You may win the argument, but you'll lose the customer in the process. Instead, show empathy. Tell the buyer you understand how he or she feels and that together you're going to find a solution to the problem.

7. *Overrelying on voice mail.* Customers who take the time to contact your company want to know there's a face behind your company. Work hard to get customers talking to your company's humans, not to its technology.

6. *Telling people "Our system is really slow today."* I hear this all the time from service representatives as they look up my record in their computer sys-tem. I realize they say this to make idle chitchat, but when they say this to me, I think to myself, What else is slow around there?

5. *Not having a FAQ on your Web site.* The frequently asked questions section of your site should cover those questions that you most frequently field from customers. More and more customers want to self-service their issues and a Web site FAQ section may just give them the immediate ser-vice they're looking for.

4. *Spending too much time with chronic complainers.* Some people will never be happy with your service. If you've received at least three complaints from the same customer, it might be time to get rid of this customer and focus on those you *can* help.

3. *Taking criticism personally.* Most callers don't want to attack you personally. Although they may be lashing out at you, they're really most frustrated by the problems they face. Take their attention off you and place it squarely back on the problems they face.

2. *Not acting like you care.* Some 68 percent of buyer defections take place because customers feel they've been treated poorly. Most customers don't expect immediate resolutions to their problems, but they do expect your concern. Routinely use phrases such as "Sorry to keep you waiting" and "Thanks for contacting us today."

1. *Not delivering what you promise.* Over time, some buyers have been continually misled by companies, so they're understandably distrustful. One of the best ways to create a standout identity is to deliver exactly what you promise. If it's "I'll call you by tomorrow with the answer" or "I'll put that in the mail today," do it. Otherwise it will ring as another false promise to an already jaded customer.

THE FOUR PILLARS OF SERVICE COOL

Without great service, your company is doomed from the start. But what exactly constitutes great service? There are four basic elements: my Pillars of Service Cool (see Figure 8.1). They are:

1. Timeliness

In today's "I want it now" society, timeliness can be a company's trump card. Yet, too many companies don't seem to respect their customers' time. Witness:

- In a recent study by Jupiter Research, 33 percent of all Internet companies surveyed took three days or longer to get back to customers who had e-mailed for help.
- A study by Portland Research Group found that the average consumer must call a company 2.3 times before having his or her issue resolved.
- Zona Research reports nearly half of all online purchases are abandoned, and a vast majority of these (more than 80 percent) are the result of delays in loading the Web pages.

Carl Sandburg once wrote that "Time is the coin of your life. Be careful lest you let other people spend it for you." We marketers would be wise to heed his advice.

FIGURE 8.1 *Pillars of Service Cool*

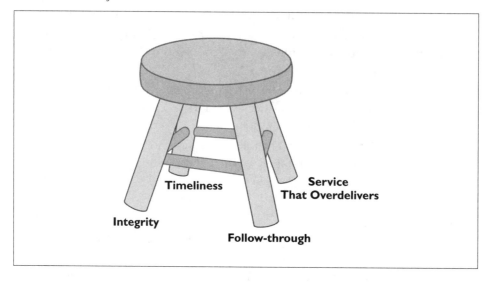

2. Servicing Customers

Too often I see companies, of all sizes, pour vast amounts of time and money into landing new customers, yet then forget about servicing these customers. To provide customers with service that keeps them coming back:

- Give them everything you contractually agreed to.
- Then give them more than what they expect.
- Keep open lines of communication throughout the relationship.
- Provide instant feedback if you expect a problem in the short term.

Provide a "postmortem" after you successfully deliver your service. Present what went well and also what could have been improved on your end.

Just as much time should be spent on delivering your product or service. Marketing efforts do not stop after the order has been placed. If you do, you risk making any new customer as angry as a bull among bumblebees.

3. Follow-through

What is a golf swing without follow-through? Accumulated energy without an outlet. A beginning without an end. Effort without results. The same is true of a company's marketing. "You can have a terrible logo and pathetic signage, but if you are known for your incredible commitment and follow-through, you will be successful," says Jim Logan, marketing consultant and popular blogger at *www.jslogan.com*. "Reverse the formula and you'll fail every time."

With diligent follow-through, your company will demonstrate its commitment, beyond a shadow of a doubt. From this, you can expect to reap repeat purchases, positive word of mouth, and referrals. These are the trifecta of successful marketing.

4. Integrity

Today's buyers are a distrustful bunch. Is it any wonder? Just look at the kinds of ethical lapses seen in today's marketing:

- In 2005, Sony Pictures Entertainment quoted the praise of a nonexistent film critic to promote several of its films. For *A Knight's Tale, The Patriot,* and several other films, plaudits were attributed to David Manning, a supposed film critic at *The Ridgeview Press.* But at the time of the reviews, *The Ridgeview Press,* a weekly in Connecticut, did not even have a film critic on staff. Sony was ordered to pay $1.5 million to settle a class-action lawsuit.
- In August of 2001, McDonald's and the FBI revealed that an employee of Simon Marketing, one of McDonald's marketing agencies, had distributed winning game pieces for the "Monopoly" and "Who Wants to Be a Millionaire" promotions to a network of accomplices. The accomplices then claimed prizes ranging from $100,000 to $1 million.
- In 2005, Abercrombie & Fitch, a favorite clothing brand among teenagers, launched a T-shirt line featuring such alcohol-related slogans as "Don't Bother, I'm Not Drunk Yet," "Bad Girls Chug, Good Girls Drink Quickly," and "Candy Is Dandy, But Liquor Is Quicker." The T-shirt line was quickly withdrawn from the market when complaints from the media and advocacy groups surfaced.

Marketers for these companies all showed an alarming lapse in ethics. To avoid blunders like these, I recommend you hold your marketers to a higher ethical standard; that's why I've created the Lipe Code of Marketing Ethics.

Don't let years of creating your company identity be wiped out in an instant by an ethical lapse. Circulate this Code of Marketing Ethics to all your marketers, and then hold them accountable for adhering to it.

LIPE'S CODE OF MARKETING ETHICS

- We will always be clear and truthful in our marketing communications.
- We will never intentionally deceive or mislead our customers. If we inadvertently do, we'll apologize—immediately.
- We will fully disclose, in large print, all pricing information.
- We will always respect the privacy of our customers.
- We will always give buyers the ability to opt out, quickly honoring their desire to do so.
- We will stand behind our products if they fail to deliver on their promises.
- We will listen to our customers' needs and concerns, and make every effort to incorporate their input.
- We will not use strong-arm tactics to get people to buy.
- We will always document claims, testimonials, and comparative statements.
- We will always accept responsibility for the consequences of our actions.

Tips for Great Telephone Service

- *Answer your telephone enthusiastically.* It sounds silly, but when you smile, your whole demeanor improves. It's as if customers feel you smiling on the other end of the line.
- *Welcome callers by identifying yourself first.* Welcome any caller with "Good morning, Cypress Technologies, Susan speaking. How may I help you?" With this basic information as a backdrop, any caller can move ahead with getting his or her request answered.
- *Always ask the caller if it's all right to put him or her on hold.* Leave every customer with the impression that he or she is the most important person in the world.
- *Provide on-hold callers with progress reports every 30 seconds.* Check back by saying, "That line is still busy. Would you like to keep holding or should I have her call you back?"
- *Don't use a speaker telephone unless absolutely necessary.* If you must use a speaker telephone, get the caller's permission first.

THE ART OF SERVING

When I tell my clients that the Latin root of the word service *(servus)* is also the root for the word *slave,* I receive some interesting reactions. But the point is there for all to see: the true art of service involves *putting the interests of your customer ahead of yours.* Do this and your company identity will stand for service. Don't and you'll come across as self-serving.

Here's an example of what I mean: One day last summer I dropped in on a well-known fast-food restaurant. On my entering the restaurant, the employee behind the counter said to me, "Hey, you, please lock the door behind you." Puzzled, I asked why. "Because I'm the only one working right now and I can't keep up," he answered. After I picked up my jaw off the ground, I pointed out that without the customers he was suggesting I lock out of the restaurant, this store may not have a business. This whole scene was so off-putting to me, to this day, I still avoid going to this location.

NO-ING YOUR CUSTOMERS

When was the last time you fired a customer? It's not easy, but it is necessary. That's because problem customers create a host of unwanted issues for your company. They tie up staff time with unnecessary demands. They spread "mind muck" such as unflattering comments or untrue statements. Many times, these problem customers end up in the "slow pay" category of your receivables operation. Don't let your company identity, which you've worked so hard to develop, be dragged down by the vile rants of problem customers. Cut them loose at once by informing them that "This is not a good fit," and then referring them to another company in your industry.

TELLTALE SIGNS YOU HAVE A PROBLEM CUSTOMER ON YOUR HANDS

It's easy to spot a problem customer once you know the telltale signs. Listen for any of these three phrases. If you ever hear these words, find a way to abandon this problem customer at once:

- *"We'll figure out how to pay for this later."* Yeah, and your company will figure out how to collect it later.

- *"We can't pay you in cash; instead, we'll give you a piece of the action."* Cash in hand beats worthless stock options any day of the week. Don't ever settle for this.
- *"We operate on a handshake."* Handshakes don't stand up in court. Insist on a purchase order, letter of agreement, or contract. A paper trail is invaluable in case your primary contact leaves the company, gets kicked upstairs, or is hit by a bus.

Some Common Customer-Service Metrics

To follow your company's customer-service improvements, track two or three of these valuable metrics:

- Total number of complaints: weekly, monthly, annually
- Complaints per total customer
- Leading types of complaints
- New types of complaints
- The age of open complaints
- Complaint resolution rates

SERVICE MARKETERS—HOW'S YOUR PACKAGING?

When a shopper picks up a product in a store, what's the first thing he or she notices? The packaging, right? The same holds true for someone buying a service. Yet instead of a folded carton with colorful graphics, *you* are the packaging for your service business. Intangible points of contact, including your clothes, your briefcase, maybe even your breath, all burn a lasting image in your buyer's mind. By paying attention to these packaging elements, you will craft the strongest company identity.

Clothes

All your technical expertise won't mean diddly if you wear a tie-dyed T-shirt and striped bell-bottoms to a client meeting. "Always dress better than you need to," says Sue Morem, author of *How to Gain the Professional Edge: Achieve the Personal and Professional Image You Want.* "Even when dealing with a casual company, remember, you are not a part of that company; you're an outsider." If you're not sure what to wear, find a personal shopping consultant.

Briefcase

I've seen people with briefcases that looked like they carried the first batch of Pony Express mail. Resist the temptation to use that briefcase Uncle Joe bought you at a rummage sale and instead invest good money in one from a reputable luggage store. Briefcases are one of the few personal effects that businesspeople carry into a meeting and this simple item speaks volumes about your image.

Your Notebook

When taking notes, do you pull out a sturdy, professional-looking notebook or just a pad of paper? This item, which sits on the table throughout the meeting, may go unnoticed by many of your buyers. Then, again, it may not.

Etiquette

Saying please and thank you. A firm handshake. Looking someone in the eye when talking to them. "Etiquette is the equivalent of the ribbon and bow on a package," says Morem. "Good etiquette lets others know you are in control and finishes off your image." For a good primer on professional etiquette, consult her book.

Proposal Covers

Early in my consulting practice, I routinely faxed my proposals to prospects. Then, one of these prospects said to me, "Jay, I have two proposals here. One is handsomely bound and the other is faxed. Which do you think I should go with?" Point taken. When final packaging your proposals or estimates, use the highest quality binding system you can afford.

E-mail Address

What image does your e-mail convey? If your e-mail address is *studmuffin@ya-hoo.com* or *hottie2468@aol.com,* you might take a step back and ask yourself, what image does this convey? If you're after a professional image for your business, and you have an e-mail address that doesn't sync with this image, you might want to consider changing your user name ("studmuffin") or even your domain name ("yahoo").

E-mail Fonts and Colors

I've received some very professional-looking e-mails. I've also received some e-mails that were laughably amateurish. These days, buyers and sellers often make initial contact through e-mail, and poorly designed e-mail templates penalize you right from the start. Use standard fonts (Courier, Times New Roman, Arial) and avoid using a background color. Consider your e-mail template as a "wrapper" for your business and treat it accordingly.

Domain Name

These days, with the costs of taking your business online dropping drastically, any small business really should have its own domain name. I'm not knocking AOL or Yahoo, but if you want to project the image of an established business that operates in a professional manner, having your own domain name is a giant leap. For more information about the availability of certain domain names, visit InterNIC at *www.internic.com.*

Voice Mail Greeting

Talk about a moment of truth for your business. The vast majority of business calls (including calls from your prospects) reach voice mail, thus underscoring the need for a professional, well-crafted greeting. Don't have your daughter recite her new poem or feature a rap version of *Auld Lang Syne.* Keep it simple and professional.

Punctuality

At the root of being on time is respect, respect for someone else's time. So be on time for all appointments. If you are running late, call and let someone know. If you're running a meeting, end on time or announce that the meeting may go longer and give anyone the opportunity to bow out.

Thinking-of-You Gestures

Stephanie Laitala is CEO of OWLL Financial *(www.owllfinancial.com)*, a $1 million company with 12 employees that specializes in part-time bookkeeping and CFO services. A voracious reader, Stephanie often clips and sends articles to clients who she knows would enjoy them, and includes a brief personal note. "I've had more clients thank me for this gesture than any other," she says. "They appreciate that I'm thinking of them. They also see that I'm committed to their business, even though I'm not the person working directly on their account. I care for them as individuals and I believe in showing it. And for my company, it's been a very successful business building tool." Wherever loyalty and caring are evident, referrals will follow.

CONCIERGE MARKETING: HOW TO TURN INFORMATION INTO A MARKETING TOOL

Buyers these days are buried in choices. A typical Google search generates millions of options. A harried grocery shopper looking for canned peaches confronts dozens of choices. What's a buyer to do? More to the point, what's a *marketer* to do?

With overstressed buyers facing a sea of information, marketers are now starting to realize that providing more information isn't the answer. Instead, more and more business owners position their companies as concierge marketers.

Take a Tip from the Concierge

Most of us are familiar with hotel concierges, the helpful souls who are stationed just inside a hotel's front door. They answer guests' questions about restaurants, shows, or other local happenings and their years of experience help guests save valuable time and money.

Some concierges are so good they end up being a point of difference for the hotel versus its competition. It's this experience *and* a company's willingness to share it that is the cornerstone of concierge marketing.

What Is a Concierge Marketer?

A concierge marketer tries to simplify a buyer's life. The concierge marketer offers a buyer helpful tips, tools, and knowledge so the buyer can navigate through the mounds of available information, cut to the chase, and make a well-informed purchase decision. The best concierge marketers put enough valuable tools in place so that the company is positioned as a wise and worldly counselor.

Some Common Concierge Marketing Tools

The first group of tools to consider as a concierge marketer is *passive tools*. These usually are printed or online informational products. Using any of these, buyers can quickly get answers to their most nagging questions. These passive tools include:

- Tip sheets
- Booklets/pamphlets
- Free downloads
- Special reports
- White papers
- Checklists
- Buying guides
- Frequently Asked Question (FAQ) sections

The Web site of the Original Mattress Factory (*www.originalmattress.com*) offers several helpful tools, including a guide to sleeping mattress dimensions and a tips section that help a buyer choose the right size mattress. At my Web site, *www.emerge-marketing.com,* I offer a "Marketing Lingo" section with more than 200 common marketing terms and their definitions.

Buyer Involvement Tools

Good concierge marketers don't just offer these passive tools and call it a day. They also offer buyer involvement tools to create dialogues with its market. Examples of buyer involvement tools are:

- Postinstallation follow-up calls
- Online customer forums
- Interactive dialogue tools

One of my favorite buyer involvement tools is Amazon.com's "Wish List" program. While at the Amazon site, I can develop my very own "Wish List" of books and then e-mail it to my family members. Using this tool, my family knows what to get me for Christmas without having to ask, so I get the Christmas presents I want, and Amazon gets the sales because it brokered this interactive transaction. Everybody saves time.

Next Steps for Concierge Marketers

If you'd like to become a concierge marketer, first identify the most common information voids your buyers face. Ask yourself these questions:

- At which stage in the buying cycle are our buyers confused?
- What information do they lack?
- What customer questions does our service staff repeatedly field?

After you identify and prioritize the answers, start designing tools to address the highest priority ones. Say, for example, your buyers are confused about which elements of your service are outsourced and which are performed in-house. The concierge marketer might then develop a FAQ section on its Web site or a PowerPoint slide that covers this topic in greater detail.

CHAPTER WRAP

Milton Hershey, founder of the Hershey Chocolate Company, once said that quality was the best kind of advertising in the world. For your company identity to be successful, your service must be of the highest quality possible. Focus on delivering world-class service first; then, and only then, consider marketing it.

9

WHAT SHOULD WE CHARGE?

Using Prices to Distinguish Your Company

What we obtain too cheap we esteem too little; it is dearness only that gives everything its value.

THOMAS PAINE

Which product feature of yours does *every* buyer ask about? Which sales tool will help close almost every sale for your company? Which feature can differentiate your company identity from most of your competitors? Your price.

Yet, despite how universally important this marketing tool is, I'm surprised at how little time businesses spend on their pricing. Here are some thoughts on setting (and getting) the right prices.

PRICE IS A PROMISE

Let's say you're grocery shopping and you come across two brands of cereal. One is a well-known brand of flakes that comes packaged in a 20-ounce box, includes a toy, and is priced at $4.99. The other is a 28-ounce store brand of flakes, packaged in a nonresealable plastic bag, that sells for $2.99. Which one would you buy?

If you based your purchase decision on price alone, you'd pick the 28-ounce bag for $2.99 and be on your way. But there's more to price than that, isn't there? There are the promises involved. In this example, the $4.99 brand promises you the highest quality ingredients and taste, an extra toy that could occupy your child while you watch reruns of *The Dick Van Dyke Show,* plus the convenience of a resealable package. And when you purchase the $4.99 brand, you get a nationally branded company that backs up its product with a 100 percent satisfaction guarantee or it'll refund your money.

Although this example deals with cereal, buyers follow similar thought patterns when examining your product or service. Every time buyers choose a product, they match up its price with its promises. So, to effectively deliver a price, you must find the promises behind your products.

DETERMINE YOUR PROMISES

As you set your prices (or consider raising them), take stock of all the *value factors* that are considered when determining your price. What attributes of your product or service are noteworthy? Following are some examples of value factors that affect the prices of products and services:

For a product:
- Quality of the raw materials
- Finished product performance
- Packaging
- On-time delivery
- Installation
- After-sale service

For a service:
- Experience level of the service provider
- Bottom-line impact of the final deliverable
- Appearance of the service provider
- Turnaround time on phone calls/e-mails
- Ability to meet deadlines

As you can imagine, your ability to deliver various factors, over and above your competitors, directly impacts the prices you set . . . and get. If you promise certain factors, but fall short on delivering them, your price will be challenged with customer complaints, delayed payments, or the loss of business to your competitors.

USE SEVERAL METHODS TO CALCULATE YOUR PRICE

One big mistake business owners make in calculating their prices is to use only one method. Although this is the easiest way, what if your calculations using this one method were wrong? (Don't laugh; the marketing world is littered with the bodies of marketing assistants who failed to catch a math error in their pricing models!) Without another pricing method to act as a cross-check, your business will be saddled with a bad price. Instead, try using several different methods to calculate prices. Here are three of the most popular:

Method #1—Costing Out a Price

The most preferred pricing calculation is called the *cost-plus method* of pricing. With this method, your company will determine all the costs that go into the product or service, then add in a desired level of profits, and combine these two numbers to arrive at a price.

To find your business's total costs, you must account for two cost types: *direct costs* and *indirect costs*. *Direct costs* are those incurred when delivering your service and typically include labor and materials. For example, if you owned a T-shirt store, your direct costs would include the labor to staff the store, the blank T-shirts you buy from a vendor, the decals you apply to the shirts, and all the equipment you use to apply the decals to the shirts.

Indirect costs are all other costs not accounted for in your direct costs and include such things as rent, insurance, phone and utility bills, and office supplies. These indirect costs cover everything you need to keep your business operating every day, *whether or not you make a sale.*

After you've determined all your direct and indirect costs, total them up. Let's say your costs for a T-shirt business are $10,000 annually. You estimate you can sell 2,000 T-shirts in a year. Dividing your $10,000 in expenses by the 2,000 quantity, you end up with a breakeven of $5 per T-shirt. This *breakeven price* is the lowest price you can charge and still cover all your costs.

The next step is to ask yourself what profit you want. Let's say you'd like to have $20,000 to live on during the year (not a princely sum, but I am just trying to keep this simple). This is your *profit*. OK, now take that $20,000 and divide it by the 2,000 T-shirts you expect to sell, and you come up with $10 per T-shirt. Add this to your $5 per T-shirt cost and the price you should charge is $15 per T-shirt.

Method #2—Pricing Competitively

After you've established your cost-based price, you want to compare this price against market prices. These are prices your competitors are already getting, and will act as a reality check for your cost-based price.

Finding competitive information isn't all that hard; it just takes a little digging. If I were the owner of the T-shirt store, I would visit five other T-shirt shops and ask for the prices of their T-shirts. Then I'd determine if each of them offers the same quality T-shirts as I do. If their prices were higher, I'd be pressed to find out what else they were offering to justify that higher price. If their prices were lower, I'd wonder if their product quality (or service) was noticeably lower. This kind of competitive surveillance is crucial when determining your prices.

What if your company sells services instead? Where can you find competitive pricing information? Here are some common sources of information:

- Your best customers can supply you with competitive price sheets.
- Trade associations might monitor pricing among the trade.
- Job candidates interviewing with your company—who come from competitors.

Method #3—Pricing by Position

Now, set your calculator aside and ask yourself this question, "How do we want our company to be perceived in the market?" This is an important question because your prices position your service (or product) in your prospects' minds. What do I mean by this? Think Ferrari. Now think Ford. Totally different price points, totally different perceptions, right?

If you want to be positioned as the higher end (think Ferrari), you will choose a price point towards the higher end of the price ranges already found in your market. If, on the other hand, your service is more workmanlike, sacrificing additional features and the finer touches, you'll tend to price your service lower.

In my book *The Marketing Toolkit for Growing Businesses,* I identify at least 13 different price strategies to choose from. To make things easier, I've condensed your choices to these three:

1. Premium price (most expensive third of your market)
2. Middle market price (midlevel third of your market)
3. Budget price (least expensive third of your market)

Depending on the tier you choose, you will price your product or service in that third of the market. For example, if you choose middle market, your price(s) should fall within the middle third of all prices in your market.

A Few Words about Psychological Pricing

According to a marketing theory called *psychological pricing,* certain prices carry a positive psychological impact that can actually increase demand. In a study by the University of Chicago's Research in Marketing, the price of a container of margarine was lowered from 89 cents to 71 cents and sales volume increased 65 percent. But when that same margarine was lowered from 89 cents to *69 cents,* sales volume surged 222 percent.

Common psychological price barriers can be $20 (use $19.99) and $100 (use $99.95). If you must cross these psychological barriers in your pricing, be as careful as a nudist climbing over a barbed wire fence.

THE WORST PRICING DECISION YOU CAN MAKE

If you ever hear someone in your business say, "Right now, we need the business. Let's set our prices really low, then as we get more business, we'll raise them," then speak up. This is the *worst* pricing mistake your company can make. Why? Because you'll struggle from the outset just to cover your costs. Even if you do wind up with some profit, you'll resent working so hard for such a little payoff.

You'll also position your company in the marketplace as lower in quality versus most of your competitors (whether or not it is true). Avoid this situation at all costs and price your products correctly the first time.

WHY IT'S BETTER TO ERR ON THE SIDE OF HIGHER PRICING

If you are considering two different prices, but are unsure which to use, choose the higher one. This single move admittedly takes a lot of guts, but it will position your company's product or service as higher quality from the get-go. Plus, if you do meet resistance at this price, you now have enough margin to discount your prices to a level that your buyer finds more acceptable. The worse alternative is to choose the lower of the two prices, which leaves little room for negotiation, or profit.

THE SECOND WORST PRICING DECISION YOU CAN MAKE

Have you ever heard a sales representative say "Okay, if I lower my price to $15 a widget, will you buy?" The problem with discounting your price like this is that it communicates to any buyer that your price is overinflated. If the buyer perceives this, she will feel compelled to negotiate until she finds out what your true price is.

Instead, it's much better to couple any price discounts with an equal reduction in services or product offered. For example, you might say "Okay, I can reduce my price to $15 a widget by reducing our five-year warranty to three years." This way, you've shown flexibility in meeting the needs of your buyer, yet you've maintained your pricing integrity.

For additional pricing suggestions, see the chart in Figure 9.1.

HOW DO YOU KNOW IT'S TIME TO RAISE YOUR PRICES?

Several situations call for an immediate price increase. They are when:

- *Demand outstrips supply.* When your company is running at its full capacity (e.g., you've established three shifts, your employees incur significant overtime, or your machines are operating at full capacity), it's time to raise prices. This typically happens during a broad economic expansion.
- *Your company has taken on internal cost increases.* One rule of pricing is that costs never stay the same. If your company has taken on cost increases in the areas of wages, benefits, or other overhead costs, you may need a price increase to absorb these increases.

FIGURE 9.1 *Dos and Don'ts of Pricing*

Do	Don't
■ Err on the high side when first pricing your product or service.	■ Price low just to get the business.
■ Include *all* costs in your calculations.	■ Lower your price without taking something away.
■ Know industry standards for margins.	■ Immediately match your competitors' price advance.
■ Account for the cost of inflation in price increases.	■ Forget *all* the value bundled up in your product.
■ Add new products at higher prices.	■ Forget the cost of discounts in your final pricing analysis.
■ Be careful about discounting—often discounts are given to close a deal, but then the client forces the company to make the discount permanent.	■ Listen too much to what your sales force tells you about your pricing—for them, price is often a convenient scapegoat.
	■ Expect loyalty from an account that buys solely on price.

- *You experience external cost increases.* These can include changes in material costs, a rise in borrowing costs, increases in energy costs, or exchange-rate fluctuations.
- *Your company hasn't raised its prices in three years.* If your company hasn't raised prices in more than three years, it's likely that your margins have eroded. Costs don't stand still and neither should your prices.

If, by now, I still haven't convinced you to raise your prices, consider this: right now, your buyers are figuring out how to raise theirs!

WAYS TO COMMUNICATE A PRICE INCREASE

By far, the best way to communicate a price increase is honestly. Buyers want the straight truth, not some double-talk about why your prices are going up. Be a straight shooter about why you're raising your prices and then use any of these marketing tools to communicate with your buyers:

- Personal letters
- Day-to-day telephone calls (e.g., "I just wanted to let you know about our upcoming price increase.")
- E-mail

- Invoice stuffers
- Personal sales calls (best for very important customers)

When announcing your new prices, remind buyers of any successes you've had with them in the past. You might also educate them about recent upgrades you've made, such as purchasing advanced technology equipment or adding significant new staff. Explain, in simple terms, what factors are forcing you to raise your prices (increased raw material costs, higher exchange rates, etc.), and then encourage feedback and questions. One nice touch might be to include a list of projects (if yours is a service business) that your company could complete for the buyer under the old prices.

Don't forget to use this opportunity to retrain your staff on all the value your product or service provides. Thus, when buyers resist your higher prices (and several will), your staff can emphasize the benefits of doing business with your company, and your company stands a better chance of keeping that buyer.

LIPE'S LAW OF PRICES

It's reasonable to expect a 10 percent falloff in buyers as a result of increasing your prices. The trick throughout the whole exercise is to make sure it's the right 10 percent that go away.

SHOULD YOU EVER LOWER YOUR PRICES?

At some times, though not nearly as often as when you raise your prices, you may be forced to lower your prices. You may have excess production capacity that can't be handled through aggressive promotion. A more common situation is lowering your prices to drive out competitors, a situation I faced years ago when I managed a line of food-service products. At that time, our number one brand was a clear market leader, but it faced intense competition from newer, smaller entrants into the market. We knew these competitors' profit margins were razor thin and so couldn't follow our price decreases because of the downward pressure this would create on their margins.

I pitched the idea of lowering prices to our executive management. My rationale was that these smaller competitors would be forced to lower their prices as well and the resulting loss of revenue would force some of them out of the market. Much to my chagrin, I was laughed out of the boardroom. Years later, after I had left the company, I got my revenge when I learned through the grapevine that the company finally did lower this product's prices and, in large part, forced these competitors out of the market.

CHAPTER WRAP

Sure, pricing is a financial matter. Just as important, it's a marketing matter that defines your company identity. Because your prices will dictate your company's positioning, selling abilities, and brand, spend significant time on this standout identity element.

Part Four

THE WRITTEN WORD

Crafting an Identity That Reads Well

10

KEY MESSAGES

The Building Blocks for Smart Communications

If you're trying to persuade people to do something, or buy something, it seems to me you should use their language, the language in which they think.

DAVID OGILVY, Advertising Legend

Before you write one word of copy, I suggest you first develop several key messages that emphasize the major aspects of your company. These short, succinct statements will highlight your company's advantages and lay the groundwork for all future written communications about your company.

WHY KEY MESSAGES ARE SO IMPORTANT

Well-crafted key messages help your company stand out from the clutter for a variety of reasons. First, they signal to your market the exact kinds of audiences you're most comfortable working with. See if you don't immediately understand which audience a company is targeting with this key message:

We specialize in helping divorced dads deal with the transition.

A key message like this calls out your intended audience, and helps those readers or listeners who share these qualities identify themselves as being similar. Here's another key message that seeks to connect with a target audience:

Do you suffer from the embarrassment of hemorrhoids?

Strong key messages can also help your company underscore its unique point of difference. Here's an example of a key message that might accomplish this:

Every one of our competitors brags about their service, but we back ours up with the strongest guarantee in the industry.

Key messages also play a vital role in attracting media attention. Just listen to what one media member has to say about key messages: "When an interviewee can give me quotes that draw from their organization's key messages, I'm more likely to be their messenger," says Lucie Amundsen, a freelancer who writes a regular column for the *Minneapolis Star Tribune.* "Because quotes add a human dimension to a piece, they are very powerful. They can steer an entire story or just add a slant, but either way quotes take the writer and ultimately the reader somewhere unexpected. That's why it's time well spent working on key messages and training people to deliver them."

Because key messages are used in almost every aspect of your company's communications—with customers, prospects, vendors, employees, and even the media—they are a vital component of your company identity. After crafting your company's key messages, you'll weave them into:

- Taglines and slogans
- Brochures
- Press releases
- Press kits
- Advertisements
- Case studies
- Testimonials
- Direct-mail campaigns
- Sales presentations
- Web sites
- Media interviews

Imagine the positive impact of training all your staff on just one key message, and then turning them loose. Ten staff members delivering a memorable, consistent message in your market would have a much greater impact than 100 people spouting nonstandardized messages.

DO YOUR KEY MESSAGES PASS THE ACID TEST?

Figure 10.1 contains a quick quiz designed to test you on the strength of your company's key messages. Give yourself 1 point for each yes answer and 0 points for a no. Then grade yourself using the scoring system at the end.

FIGURE 10.1 *The Key Messages Acid Test*

1. Does your company have clearly identified key messages?

   Yes (1 point)   No (0 points)

2. Do you have at least three of them?

   Yes (1 point)   No (0 points)

3. Are they written down?

   Yes (1 point)   No (0 points)

4. Did all significant members of your company have input into their development?

   Yes (1 point)   No (0 points)

5. Does each key message reinforce a benefit that your company provides?

   Yes (1 point)   No (0 points)

6. Does at least one key message emphasize how you are different from all other competitors?

   Yes (1 point)   No (0 points)

7. Did you test the effectiveness of your key messages with a sampling of customers, vendors, employees, and media members?

   Yes (1 point)   No (0 points)

8. Did you train all company employees in using these messages immediately after developing them?

   Yes (1 point)   No (0 points)

9. Have you had at least one other key message training session since then?

   Yes (1 point)   No (0 points)

10. Does your marketing team audit how well these key messages are being used?

    Yes (1 point)   No (0 points)

Scoring system:
Points
7–10   Congratulations, you're a standout marketer.
3–6   Not bad. Try to work on key messages to stand out even more.
0–2   Oops. Your company could use a key messages makeover.

HOW TO DEVELOP KEY MESSAGES

Discover Your Buyers' Pain First

A solution to a buyer's problem is almost always grounded in that person's pain. For example, if you're about to start shopping for a new car, it may be because you worry constantly about whether your current one will start during the winter. Another example could be that you're thinking of subscribing to a newspaper for the very first time, because you're tired of not knowing what everyone is talking about on a Monday morning. Both these situations call out the pain the buyer is feeling (worrying about the car starting *and* feeling stupid around the water cooler). Effectively understanding the pain your buyers face and then translating that pain into a valid statement will help your company form an emotional bond with a buyer.

Before you ever write a word of marketing copy, first identify the pain your buyers feel. In Figure 10.2 is a list of some of the more common pain points felt by both customers and companies.

This is only a brief list. People and companies suffer from *infinite* sources of pain. To help you pinpoint your customers' pain, try asking a handful of your customers these questions:

- "When it comes to choosing a _____ (e.g., dishwasher, accounting firm, industrial manufacturer), what are the biggest challenges you face?"
- "I wish I could stop worrying about _____."
- "I'd sleep a whole lot better if only I could _____."

FIGURE 10.2 *Common Pains Felt by Customers and Companies*

Customers	**Companies**
■ Being stressed out	■ Declining sales
■ Not having enough money	■ Unprofitability
■ Feeling underappreciated	■ Poor communication
■ Not having a clear direction in life	■ Unclear strategic direction
■ Feeling unfulfilled	■ Poor image
■ Being unhappy	■ Little awareness
■ Wanting what others have	■ A staff of underperformers

Notice that the last one deals directly with sleep . . . or rather the lack of it. That's because I have found that sleep is one of mankind's most treasured possessions. If you can identify what keeps your buyers up at night (that your product or service solves), then your company will be a hero in that person's mind.

FOCUS ON BENEFITS

In Chapter 2 I emphasized how important it is to use benefits in your marketing communications, but it bears repeating. Benefits are one of the most powerful marketing weapons at your disposal because they illustrate exactly how your buyers' lives are made better after purchasing your product.

Benefits, correctly used, will persuade and motivate buyers to seek out your company. But if you don't communicate about your benefits, your buyers will be left wondering why they should buy from you. If you're still unclear what benefits are and how to use them, read Commandment VI in Chapter 2 again.

An Ode to Benefits

I see that you've spent quite a big wad of dough
To tell me the things you think I should know.
How your plant is so big, so fine, and strong;
And your founder has whiskers so handsomely long.
So he started the business in old '92?
How tremendously int'resting this is—to YOU.
He built up the thing with the blood of his life?
I'll run home like mad, tell that to my wife.
Your machinery's modern and, oh, so complete!
Your rep is so flawless, your workers so neat.
Your motto is "Quality"—capital "Q."
No wonder I'm tired of "your" and "you."
So tell me quick and tell me true.
(Or else, my friend, to heck with you!)
LESS: How this product came to be.
MORE: What the darn thing DOES FOR ME!
—Anonymous

SOME HINTS ON DEVELOPING EFFECTIVE KEY MESSAGES

- *Keep them short.* Each key message should be one sentence long and take no more than five seconds to say.
- *Be honest.* Key messages must align with the reality of your service. If your service saves customers time, say it. But if you know that your service involves a steep learning curve, stay away from any key messages that might refer to how easy it is.
- *Offer proof.* Back up your key messages, wherever possible, with proof. If you can show that "Ninety-nine percent of our customers are delighted with our product," that makes for a better key message than "Our customers are satisfied."
- *Keep them positive.* Good key messages talk about what you can do, not what you can't.
- *Avoid jargon.* Jargon makes one set of buyers feel confused and another set feel stupid. Neither makes for good marketing results.

CHAPTER WRAP

Crafting solid key messages up front, before you write a word of copy, will make creating the rest of your marketing communications that much easier. If you shortcut this important process, though, you risk sending out inconsistent or confused messages into the market. Spend quality time crafting standout key messages first; then, and only then, move ahead to the next step of writing copy.

11

HOW TO WRITE COPY THAT MOTIVATES PEOPLE TO BUY

The greatest problem with communication is the illusion that it has been accomplished.

GEORGE BERNARD SHAW

All the money you've poured into getting the word out on your company, all the hours your sales force has invested in meeting with and presenting to buyers will go to waste if your marketing copy sucks. It's that simple.

If the words you use to describe your company and what it offers are poorly chosen, inconsistent with your company brand, or amateurish, buyers won't emotionally connect with your company. But if you feature crisp, clear, and compelling copy in all your communications, your company identity will benefit in many ways, including:

- Demonstrating to buyers you have experience solving their problems
- Articulating exactly what makes your company unique from others
- Building strong bonds of trust with buyers
- Directly addressing the doubts buyers have about doing business with you
- Raising the confidence buyers have in your company

- Telling buyers exactly what they should do next
- Showing how your company does a superior job
- Strengthening a customer's loyalty

GOOD EXAMPLES OF BAD COPY

Before I talk about how to write good marketing copy, here are a few examples of bad copy. Each one of these has been taken from an actual company's marketing materials:

- *Corporate decision makers now stand at the tip of the spear of an increasingly complex flow of information.* (The writer mixes too many metaphors here. Does anyone stand at the "tip of a spear"? What relevance is there between the tip of a spear and the "increasingly complex flow of information"?)
- *Due diligence cries out for clarification, verification, and confirmation of critical information and processes used for its generation.* (I'd be hard-pressed to find a better example of "gobbledygook prose" than this.)
- *Matched with health care industry experience, you will find additional potential value displayed in skills acquired through acquisition of certifications as a Certified Fraud Examiner (CFE), a Fellow of the Healthcare Financial Management Association (FHFMA) and an ATM-Silver in Toastmasters.* (Why not just say, "I have the health care experience you're looking for and the following certifications"?)
- *My efforts in winning recognition as a data detective treat each effort as a new beginning. As one new to this activity, I am eager to build a reputation through provision of a unique and superior service. You could expect me to bring this commitment to all services performed.* (How can I trust you to be the expert in this field if you're "new to this activity"?)
- *I am actively seeking additional members in The XYZ Group and could really use your assistance in achieving my growth objectives.* (This is a classic example of "All about Me" copy. The writer assumes I'm as jazzed about helping him achieve his growth objectives as he is. I'm not.)

PICKING THE RIGHT VOICE FOR YOUR COMPANY

Every bit of copy has a voice, or a tone, to it. The same ten words, said using different voices, can generate different reactions. In the following examples, I've written the same thought using three different voices:

1. *"Don't miss out on this opportunity."* (Here I'm authoritative.)
2. *"We don't want you to miss out on this opportunity."* (Here I'm helpful.)
3. *"Only an idiot would pass up this opportunity."* (And here I'm, well, downright condescending.)

See what I mean about how different tones can affect just ten words? So, before you start writing any copy at all, pick which voice you want for your company. Here are some voices you could choose for your company's marketing content:

- Kind
- Helpful
- Prestigious
- To the point
- Urgent
- Professional
- Smart
- Honest
- Friendly
- Energetic
- Enthusiastic
- Supportive
- Exclusive
- Authoritative
- Approachable
- Creative
- Cool
- Avant-garde

AN EXAMPLE OF USING THE WRONG TONE

Here is the first paragraph of a sales letter I received recently. See if you don't agree with the thoughts that ran through my head (in brackets) as I read it. Listen carefully for the tone it presents:

Dear Jay,

I wanted to take this opportunity to introduce myself [Seems a bit forward—kind of like barging into another's conversation]. *My name is Nick _____, and I am your Account Representative from ABC Business Systems* [I didn't know I had an account with you, Nick]. *We offer many unique imaging systems that have applications that would be beneficial to your organization* [What do you *know* about my organization?].

In my view, this letter clubs me over the head with a superior tone from the outset, like the insurance salesman at a cocktail party who launches into a sales pitch right after hearing "Hi, what's your name?" In short, it presumes too much in too short a time.

A better first paragraph, in my opinion, would have started with "Is your organization's copier on its last leg? Are you constantly hunting down maintenance people to fix your computer?" Starting a letter with questions like these doesn't presume anything. Rather, it puts the reader in the driver's seat to either agree or disagree, then earns the right to talk authoritatively later on.

AVOID THE I–ME–MINE APPROACH TO COPYWRITING

One day, my 11-year-old son announced that he wanted a GameCube game system, so I made a deal with him. If he developed a brochure that would sell me on the idea, then I would buy him the system.

His first attempt at this brochure was a petition that stated he really needed a GameCube and it was signed by all his classmates. As you can imagine, I took a dim view of this. After I explained to him that he needed to relate to *my* interests as the purchaser, rather than *his* as the buyer, he came up with a second, much more effective approach. He talked to the father of one of his buddies who already owned a GameCube and asked him to explain how the GameCube made the dad's life easier. The dad said such things as, "It keeps my son occupied so I can get more work done," and "He can invite his friends over and have more things to do with them."

After my son put these thoughts into a homemade "brochure" and presented it to me, I was more impressed. This time, he had looked at the challenge from the buyer's perspective (mine), not his own. Needless to say, I bought him the GameCube on the strength of this effort.

Too many companies use the I–Me–Mine approach, generating content that covers why they are the best at something, rather than why buyers should be interested. One of the greatest challenges in my line of work is getting clients to see that marketing efforts, focused on the buyers' perspective, are so much more effective.

TOP TEN COPYWRITING TIPS

10. *Seek to communicate personally, even in a mass communication.* Develop any marketing piece with the sense that you're writing a personal letter to just one reader. It's a variation on the advice singers are given to try to sing to just one person in a crowd.

9. *Hold your reader's attention.* A recent study by the U.S. Postal Service found that 64 percent of households don't really mind an influx of direct-mail packages as long as they are kept interesting.

8. *Know the ins and outs of what you're writing about.* No one can convincingly sell a service he or she knows little about. Try, or better yet, *use* the product yourself. There's no better way to communicate authentically than when you know what you're talking about.

7. *Spend time with your headline.* Direct-marketing research has shown that the headline, the very first thing the reader encounters, is responsible for close to 80 percent of a marketing ad's response. Given this fact, do you spend anywhere near this amount of time on your headline when developing your marketing materials?

6. *Tell your reader exactly what you want him or her to do next.* The goal of every marketing piece should be to generate a response. The call to action, a block of copy that tells your reader *exactly* what to do next, gets the reader to take the right next step. If you don't provide this very basic information, your reader will finish your marketing piece and very likely move on to something else, without taking any action.

5. *Avoid hyperbole.* I've noticed more and more exaggeration creep into companies' marketing efforts. For example, I recently heard one company refer to its service as the "best on the planet." I realize this is supposed to be funny, but how many of your prospects will see it that way? Avoid statements like:
   - World's best . . .
   - The biggest . . .
   - The King of . . .
   - The area's only . . .
   - We're number one.

4. *Use active verbs and language.* In marketing, there's no place for the verb *to be*. Instead of writing "Our service is designed to improve your productivity," use "Our software improves your productivity."

3. *Single out your desired audience.* This approach is used in seminar mailings that include a "Who Should Attend" section. Calling out a person's title or department is an effective way of getting readers to qualify themselves for your product or service. Once they see that you're talking to people just like them, they take a more personal interest in what you're saying.

2. *Check before publishing*. Friends, spouses, grandparents, children, maybe even the dog (if it's an especially smart one) should review your copy before it ever hits a printing press. I'm lucky because my chief proofreader is my wife, a person who doesn't come from the ranks. As a result I can count on her to give me the unvarnished truth about what I've written.

1. *Test, test, and retest*. Good marketers are never satisfied. That's why they constantly test, test, and retest copy. They may change the opening paragraph of a letter, experiment with a new headline, or vary the offer in the P.S. Whatever the variable that is tested (a sentence, a paragraph, a new letter), the good marketer spends time trying to find a better copy approach.

Tips on Typestyles

Here are some rules of thumb for typestyle use from Colin Wheildon's excellent book, *Type & Layout: Are You Communicating or Just Making Pretty Shapes?*

- *Use serif type for all body copy.* Serif type (Times New Roman) scored much higher on reading comprehension tests than sans serif (Arial). In fact, 67 percent of readers had good comprehension level of serif type, yet only 12 percent had the same comprehension for sans serif type.

- *The darker the headline, the greater the comprehension level.* Headlines in black type were understood by nearly *four times* as many readers as brightly colored headlines were.

- *Headlines read better without a period.* By adding a period to a headline, comprehension levels drop 13 percent.

- *Do not use all caps for headlines.* Headlines in all capital letters are significantly harder to read than those set in uppercase and lowercase. In an experiment, headlines were set in five different typestyles (Roman Old Style, Roman Modern, Sans Serif, Optima, and Square Serif) and then shown to readers in both ALL CAPS format and uppercase and lowercase format. A vast majority of readers, for every single typestyle, preferred the uppercase and lowercase headlines.

THREE OF THE MOST EFFECTIVE DEVICES TO GET BUYERS TO ACT

Supply Scarcity

In Robert Chialdini's book *Influence: The Psychology of Persuasion*, he makes a compelling argument for using scarcity as a communication tactic. As most of us know, anything that is rare, or becoming rarer, is valued more by consumers. That's why a Honus Wagner baseball card is more valuable than a Roger Clemens one. It's also why a limited-edition painting commands a higher price. And it's why Disney rereleases older films on DVD for a limited time, before the company "returns them to the vault." Good marketers understand this principle and use communications such as:

- Only six seats remain (scarcity of supply).
- Buy now before prices rise (scarcity of time).
- Salespeople will be in your area only on Friday (scarcity of promotion).

Window of Availability

I once sat on a discussion panel for small business marketers and learned how one of my fellow panel members had used scarcity of time in a communication of hers. Because several of her projects were scheduled to end at the same time, she saw an upcoming period when her business would be quiet. So she e-mailed her database the following message:

> Hi! I'm just finishing up several big projects and see that I might have some additional time available in the next two weeks. Do you have a project you're trying to get to and just can't? Maybe I can help . . .

The response to her e-mail was immediate. Several new clients approached her asking about her services and one of her existing clients (whose project she was wrapping up) contacted her about another project. The result? More work than she could handle.

Peer Pressure

Recently, I received in the mail a printer's proof of donors to my MBA class of 1987. Listed in class order were all the donors to my graduate school, Northwestern University's Kellogg School of Management. Stenciled across this tabloid-style newspaper was the word "Proof," and the copy "Is your name not listed and you would like it to be? It is not too late." was found in the mouse type further down the page.

This approach uses peer pressure as a prime motivator. I'm gently nudged because it points out which of my peers have beaten me to the punch of donating to my alma mater. Yet, all is not lost because there is still a chance for me to donate and catch up with my peers. I think to myself, Hmmm, Steve Johnson gave and I know he's out of a job, or Alice Needham gave? I thought she was in the Peace Corps. For many people, peer pressure is the greatest motivational force. Try weaving this approach into your marketing copy.

YOUR COPY MUST SOLVE A PRESSING PROBLEM

For a riding mower, a buyer's most pressing problem might be "I spend too much of my weekend mowing the lawn." For a landscape gardening service, the problem might be "I don't know how to make my lawn look as good as my neighbor's." Whatever your product or service, you have to uncover the most nagging problem confronting your buyers. Once you discover what this is, shape all your marketing copy around the notion that you have the solution to this vexing problem.

THE THREE BIGGEST NO-NO'S OF WRITING COPY

1. *Lying to your audience.* In August of 2005, *USA Today* ran a feature on the president of Hat Trick Beverage, a $5 million maker of distinctive beverages. In the article, the company's president, Larry "Buzzy" Twombly, was profiled as a man who graduated from Harvard, played hockey for three separate minor-league teams, and was drafted by the Boston Bruins professional hockey team. The trouble was that none of this was true. Twombly knowingly fabricated these credentials because he thought it would get him more coverage. Well, it did. Only it wasn't the kind of coverage he was looking for. Immediately after these falsehoods were discovered, *USA Today* published another story detailing the elaborate charade. Millions of people now know this man to be a liar. Imagine how hard it will be for him to get media coverage for this company, or any other company of his in the future. Don't undo years of hard work because of a "little white lie."

LIPE'S LAW OF COPYWRITING

Do Away with the Zingers

We marketers have to be careful not to overuse exclamation points (or "zingers" as they're sometimes called). In the process of trying to communicate excitement, we may overreach and communicate something entirely different—like desperation. Limit your use of zingers to once every couple of pages. Otherwise you'll leave readers with the impression that you're trying too hard.

---

2. *Not breaking up your copy visually.* One of the first things a reader does when confronted with a page of copy is ask, "Is this going to be worth the effort to read?" To help him or her answer yes, use any (or all) of these devices to make your copy more approachable:

   • Bullet points
   • Drop caps
   • Indenting lines
   • Sidebars
   • Photographs

3. *Not including contact information on every page.* Your company's name, address, telephone number(s), e-mail address(es), and Web site should appear on *every* page of your marketing materials. Even if it's your eight-page brochure. The next time you're leafing through a catalog, see if this isn't true. These super-sophisticated marketers realize that large numbers of people tear out pages from a catalog and toss the rest of the catalog away. With the contact information at the bottom of every page of your marketing materials, you still make it easy for buyers who "slice and dice" your materials.

A REAL-LIFE EXAMPLE OF CONTACT INFORMATION THAT WAS LACKING

One day last spring I noticed that spyware and adware had slowed my computer to a crawl. So I pulled out a flyer from a local company that performs on-site computer services. As I scanned the flyer, I saw a listing of services they provide and a comprehensive price list. The flyer even sported a cute logo in the upper left-hand corner. But then I tried for the next five minutes to find a telephone number to call for a service appointment. No luck. Someone forgot to put a telephone number, e-mail address, or even a Web site address on the flyer. *Not one stitch* of contact information was listed to help me take the next step.

Buyers these days are too busy to hunt around for a telephone number. We want *all* the information *now*. Do your business a favor and make sure every piece of your company literature contains complete contact information.

A TIP FOR PROOFREADING YOUR COPY

One day when I was a marketer at General Mills, I stumbled past the packaging department and saw something that I will never forget. Two of the packaging directors were seated facing each other, each holding a package flat for a brand-new product, *reading out loud to each other*. When I asked another person in the department why they were doing this, she answered that they were final proofing the package copy. Because each package is seen by millions of consumers, they had learned long ago that reading the copy to each other was a foolproof way to catch many errors.

Ever since that day, I've insisted that all my clients final proof their copy by reading it out loud. If you adopt this method, not only will you catch typos, but you'll also discover those bits of copy that are a bit rough around the edges. Try this approach once, and I guarantee you'll be sold on it.

CHAPTER WRAP

There's no question that it's a blast to chew over brand-new Web site templates, updated brochure layouts, or new logo designs. But the fact is that the words you use to communicate with your buyers are what will make the cash register ring. These words craft images in your buyers' minds and help your company connect emotionally with them. Remember this as you begin writing copy for a marketing vehicle. Your buyers must see the right words to feel comfortable parting with their hard-earned money.

12

TESTIMONIALS

A Terrific Trust-Building Tool

There are two kinds of people in this world: those who come into a room and say,
"Well, here I am!" and those who say, "Ah, there you are."

FREDERICK COLLINS, Author

I t's hard to deny that today's buyers are a distrustful bunch. But if some of your marketing messages come directly from the mouths of your customers, buyers may be more apt to listen. Testimonials from your satisfied customers are a terrific way to build confidence about doing business with your company.

WHY EVERY COMPANY SHOULD USE TESTIMONIALS

Prominently featuring testimonials will help your company's identity by:

- *Building bonds of trust.* Tooting your own horn can sometimes undermine the credibility of your marketing efforts. To build stronger bonds of trust with your company, let others do the tooting. When a buyer reads a testimonial about your company, it's considered objective feedback and therefore seen as more trustworthy.

- *Improving credibility.* A client of mine sells telecommunications services to Fortune 500 companies. Yet, nowhere in their materials do the names of these Fortune 500 companies appear. This is a mistake. Prospects, especially Fortune 500 companies, want to know you've worked with companies like theirs in the past.

Sometimes when I mention this, an executive chirps up and asks, "Why would we want to tip off our competitors about who our clients are?" The answer is that you risk more by *not* doing so. If you don't do everything you can to reassure your buyers that doing business with your company is the best decision they could make, they'll take their business elsewhere. Almost every act within your marketing efforts involves taking calculated risks, and featuring testimonials from satisfied customers is a risk well worth taking.

Demonstrate Success

First-time buyers want to work with successful companies—hoping a little of that success rubs off on them. Read this next testimonial and ask yourself if it doesn't make you want to do business with this company:

> *XYZ Laundry Supply was there from day one, all the way to final build-out of our Laundromat. They took the time to teach me everything I needed to know about this business. Now that my first coin laundry is open, I'm looking to open another and I feel like XYZ and I are on a mission together.*

THE TWO TYPES OF TESTIMONIALS— UNSOLICITED AND SOLICITED

There are two kinds of testimonials—unsolicited and solicited. *Unsolicited testimonials* are those that arrive at your doorstep, without any effort on your part. The buyer took it upon herself to contact you directly with her story. Here are some ways you can expect to receive unsolicited testimonials:

- E-mail
- Snail mail letters
- Random conversations (either over the telephone or in person)

Keep a file folder of these unsolicited testimonials. Then, when the time is right, break them out and sprinkle them liberally throughout your marketing materials.

Solicited testimonials are those you consciously pursue through devices such as:

- Comment cards
- Warranty cards
- Postpurchase surveys or telephone calls
- Web site "Contact us" sections
- Blog comment sections

In my work with hundreds of businesses, I've found that 90 percent of the testimonials for these companies are solicited. Thus, if you want testimonials from your marketing efforts, you must put some time and effort into obtaining them (like everything else in your marketing effort).

WHO WRITES THEM—YOU OR THEM?

I am asked this question a lot and the answer is *you* should write them. Why? Because if you leave it up to your customers, it just won't get done. They have more important things on their to-do lists. The right way to get testimonials from your customers is for you to write two different testimonials for them, and then let them choose which one they prefer. After you've drafted the two testimonials, also include a section called "I Can Do Better Than That" and leave some blank space for them to write their own testimonial. Put both of these sections on a single-sided sheet of paper and send it to them. Figure 12.1 shows what a testimonial draft sheet might look like.

With a format like this, if the customer likes what you've written, all he does is sign and return the form to you. If he feels moved to write his own testimonial, though, he can do that on the same page. One important note: from my experience, whenever satisfied clients write their own testimonials, they are *always* better than the ones you could write. I predict that you'll be surprised at how insightful and eloquent your customers will be.

Another thing: if you have sales representatives in your company, get them involved in obtaining these testimonials. They'll cherish the opportunity to reconnect with satisfied customers, and these opportunities may become learning moments for the sales reps as they find out firsthand why customers turn to your company.

FIGURE 12.1 *Sample Testimonial Draft*

XYZ COMPANY

Testimonial Draft Sheet

I like this one:

☐   *"Every time I pull a pair of Fasthand Drum Sticks out of their sleeves, I know they'll perform exactly like all the others I've used."*

OR

☐   *"Because these Fasthand Drum Sticks are durable and light, I give my best performance night after night."*

I can do better than that:

Name _____

Signature _____

Company _____

Date _____

WHAT SHOULD A TESTIMONIAL SAY?

In my experience, the most convincing testimonials focus on communicating, in no uncertain terms, one central idea. That idea should revolve around a specific aspect of your business (or product or service) and nothing more. Here are some examples of testimonials that concentrate on one central idea:

- *Company specific.* "How does XYZ help me? They improve my store image by keeping my machines up and running. Nothing hurts your store image more than broken machines."
- *Person specific.* "Phil Jones was Johnny-on-the-spot. Every time I needed help, he was either on-site in less than an hour or he counseled me over the phone."
- *Product or brand specific.* "We've had U-Clean-Ems for over 15 years. Pound for pound, they're the best machines on the market."
- *Service specific.* "One Friday at 5 PM, I called Spritz Cleaners in a panic. Not only did they answer their phone, but they got a service truck out here within 15 minutes. You can't beat service like that."

THREE THINGS EVERY TESTIMONIAL MUST HAVE

1. A name at the bottom. The more your testimonials have names attached to them, the better. They're just more believable this way. Plus, there's an outside chance the reader of the testimonial knows the person who wrote it. When this happens, very often the two individuals will talk about your company, with the reader asking the testimonial provider, "Is this really true what you said about XYZ Company?" In this example (which has happened numerous times for my business and my clients' businesses), the testimonial is actually encouraging word of mouth for your business.

2. An emotion. Which of these testimonials does a better job of involving the reader?

- *"Wow, was I surprised. I never thought I could get my accounting questions answered so quickly."*
- *"I got my accounting questions answered quickly."*

Wouldn't you agree that the first testimonial, because of the underlying emotion in it, actually draws in a reader better?

3. A definable benefit. In any testimonial, the reader must see a clear benefit to what your company offers. For example, it's not enough for a testimonial to say: *"He really knows his stuff."* Instead, the head-turning testimonial says: *"He knows his stuff so well, he saved me over 20 hours of my own time."*

This second one points out the tangible results—the end benefit of working with this person—and makes for a much more attention-grabbing quote. Using this same logic, which of the two following quotes carries more impact?

- *"XYZ's service helped us launch three new initiatives and save a week's worth of management time."*
- *"They really helped us a lot."*

LIPE'S LAW OF TESTIMONIALS

Every testimonial for your company should be three sentences or less. Each sentence should have 15 words or less. Less is more.

ONE LAST IDEA FOR OBTAINING TESTIMONIALS

Clients often ask me, "How do I actually get testimonials from satisfied clients after we've finished working together?" My reply is that you should be asking for them much sooner in the relationship—like right at the beginning. Why not put a clause in your contract that makes obtaining a testimonial a standard part of doing business with your company? It could look like this:

After completing the project, and obtaining your approval, [your company] would like to feature our work together in a testimonial.

A contract clause like this sets the expectation, at the very beginning of the relationship, that a testimonial will be expected immediately after the project or purchase is complete.

CHAPTER WRAP

In judicial systems, a testimony is a solemn statement, made under oath, that authenticates a fact. Testimonials do much the same for your business. Not only do they authenticate facts, but they sway opinion. Incorporating testimonials into your company's materials will prove, beyond a shadow of a doubt, that your company has a standout identity.

TRIED-AND-TRUE TOOLS

*Your Company's Make-or-Break
First Impressions*

13

YOUR COMPANY'S NAME

The Most Crucial First Impression

A good name is more desirable than great riches.

PROVERBS 22:1

How different would you be if your name were Clem or Matilda? What if your name were Rex or Mercedes? Your personal name sets the tone for almost every interaction you have in your life, and a company name is just as important for the same reason. If your company name is intriguing or likable, your marketing messages will carry that much more weight. If it's weak or confusing, though, the rest of your marketing efforts will be watered down.

Read on and learn how to create a company name that is distinctive, memorable, and protectable.

NAME—A FIRST TOUCHPOINT

Company reputations are made or lost on first impressions, and in many instances, your company's name will make the first impression. Buyers might hear it during a casual conversation, see it on a trade show booth, view it on the front cover of a brochure, or hear it during a radio commercial. There are literally hundreds of ways a buyer will first hear your company name. You must ensure your name sets the right tone for your company identity from the moment your buying audience first learns about it.

FOUR THINGS YOUR COMPANY NAME MUST BE

1. Appealing

If one goal of your company identity is to create positive associations with buyers, then it naturally holds that your name must carry a wide appeal. You don't want to risk turning off buyers right at the moment they learn of your company name. One way to measure the appeal of a company name is to ask ten people the question, "What do you think of when you hear the word _____ [your company name]?" This kind of technique will help elicit others' feelings about your name, including any hidden connotations, double entendres, or limitations.

2. Memorable

Whatchamacallit is not the name you want people to remember your company by. Unless you craft a company name that's easy to remember, you may well end up with this default name. One of the best ways to test the memorability of any company name is to use a simple recall test. Read a list of six company names (one of which is yours) to a person and then, after a short while, ask him to repeat as many of the names as he can. If your name is chosen, your name gets a vote for memorability. To test visual memorability, *show* the person a list of six names rather than saying them out loud.

3. Succinct

According to the book *Crafting the Perfect Name* (Alder Press, 1995), the popularity of company name lengths, by number of words, is:

Two words	9%
Three words	50%
Four words	35%
Five or more words	6%

Combine this information with the fact that almost two-thirds of all corporate name changes involve *shortening* the name and you have an argument for keeping your company name short and sweet. Some names are shortened because a company outgrows its original core competency (e.g., Minnesota Mining and Manufacturing was shortened to 3M as it expanded past mining). The point remains: a shorter name creates more impact and requires the buyer to remember less. And a shorter company name is easier to fit on letterheads, brochures, trade show banners, signs, Web sites, and most other marketing materials.

4. Easy to Find

Where in the telephone book do you look for companies named *2 Close for Comfort, 3rd Lair Skate Park*, and *4* Com? More important, how do you spell their Web site URLs? Twocloseforcomfort.com or 2closeforcomfort.com? Thirdlair.com or 3rdlair.com? Fourcom or 4com? A winning company name shouldn't leave any doubt in a buyer's mind about how it's spelled or where it would be found in a directory listing.

TEN WAYS TO NAME YOUR COMPANY

1. Benefit-oriented Names

Examples: U-Haul, Emerge Marketing
Whether you're developing a company name or a product name, singling out a specific benefit within the name itself is an excellent method. Here are three examples of company names that feature benefits:

- Sprint
- U-Haul
- Budget Car Rental

For each of these company names, no one has to work very hard to understand what the brand stands for. Just for fun, here are the names of each of their chief competitors: Eschelon, Koch National Lease, and Americar. What do *they* stand for? Don't ask me, because I don't know. The benefit approach to naming establishes quickly in your prospects' minds *who* you are and *what* you do. Use it if you can.

2. Invented Names

Examples: Intel, Exxon, Compaq

These names don't actually mean anything, but they *are* easier to protect and that explains their growing popularity. Certain names using this method will be distinctive, but will they be as memorable? Even though such a name may be easier to protect, you'll want to make sure that the name promotes the desired image.

3. Combination Names

In *Crafting the Perfect Name,* authors George Burroughs Blake and Nancy Blake-Bohne outline a simple process for generating a company name. First, they divide the name into three sections: the *distinctive* part of the name (who), the primary *activity* of the company (what), and the *type* of organization (what kind).

Then they suggest brainstorming various word options for each section. Using a fictitious example, your options table might look like this:

Distinctive Name (Who)	Activity (Does what)	Type of Organization (What kind)
Aldrich	Marketing	Company
Dunleavy	Research	Associates
Aplomb	Real Estate	Corporation
Keynote	Payroll Processing	International
Success	**Software**	**Partners**
Reach	Knowledge	Group

Now using this grid, you'd choose the best word option in each section and combine them into a company name. In this example, I've generated *Keynote Software Partners* as a possible company name.

4. Founders' Names

Examples: Johnson & Johnson, Hewlett-Packard

Today our business world is quite different than it was just 30 years ago. In those days, you could name your company Hewlett-Packard and stand a chance of breaking through the clutter. Today, I don't think you can. There are just too many messages clamoring for attention. The name Hewlett-Packard, standing on its own, doesn't help describe the business you're in, nor the benefits you offer, so I don't generally recommend this approach.

There *are* a couple caveats to this. If you're a famous personality with equity already built into your name (e.g., Henry Kissinger & Associates), then this approach makes sense. Also, in certain professions (legal and accounting come to mind), it's an established practice to use the names of the founders. However, if you can come up with a good name using another method, I would.

5. The Dreaded "& Associates"

Examples: Too numerous to count

I meet with a lot of folks who are just launching new companies. They proudly take me through their business ideas, and then slide business cards across the table. My heart sinks, though, when I read, for example, *Joe Blow & Associates*. Instead of working hard for a distinctive name, this owner instead chose the dreaded "& Associates" name. I'll probably get a lot of people's noses out of joint by saying this, but naming your company after yourself is a mistake. The "& Associates" typically connotes you're just starting out, and five years from now, if you have ten employees, you'll still be communicating "small" to the market. Plus, this name just doesn't show any creativity.

6. The Power of Alliteration

Examples: The Teeming Turnip, Emerge Marketing, and Coca-Cola

Alliteration is using the same sound or syllable in succession. This technique is a powerful way to impart cadence to a name and, thus, improve its memorability. Not only will you find many company names that use this technique, but it's also a widely used practice in naming cartoon characters: Peter Piper, Donald Duck, Mickey Mouse, Minnie Mouse, Super Sonic, Woody Woodpecker, Clark Kent, and Lois Lane.

7. Mythological Names

Examples: Midas Muffler, Ajax Cleaner

Mythological names tap a rich vein of imagery already in a buyer's mind. By choosing a mythological character that embodies the qualities you want in your company identity, you'll draw on the heritage of that name.

8. Alphabet Soup

Examples: IBM, ABC, FMC

Using an acronym to name your company is my least favorite method, yet it still seems to be popular these days. Many times this approach is used as a fallback position because a company has expanded past its original core competency. IBM (International Business Machines) and GE (General Electric) are two good examples of companies whose offerings have expanded well past their original names. As a result, they have shortened their company names to initials instead.

I generally don't recommend this approach because alphabet soup names like these (without the benefit of millions of advertising dollars each of these companies enjoys) aren't particularly distinctive or memorable. If you've outgrown your company name, or most people in the market are using an abbreviated version of your name (e.g., your company, Industrial Plastics Corporation, is commonly referred to as IPC), it might be time to freshen your identity.

9. Blending Two Different Words

Examples: KitchenAid, Adjustastroke, WaterPik

Sometimes blending two different words can produce a winning name. The objective is to find the right two words that describe the business your company is in, then mesh them together. For example, the product name WaterPik took two different words—*water* and *toothpick*—and blended them together. The resulting name not only communicates what the product is, but is also catchy to say.

10. Going for Humor

Examples: Banana Republic, Hang Ten, L'eggs

Sometimes a humorous name can give you an edge in the marketplace. A hair salon near where I live is called "Curl up and Dye." And just look at all the musical bands who take this approach to naming:

- *Fine Young Cannibals*
- *10,000 Maniacs*
- *Crash Test Dummies*
- *Captain Zimbabwe and the Cabinet Shuffle*
- *String Cheese Incident*
- *Oingo Boingo*

These are all real bands that have turned their band names into marketing assets. A word of caution: sometimes humor can be achieved at the expense of other individuals, organizations, or groups. If you use a humorous naming approach, be careful that the final name you choose doesn't alienate anyone.

A FEW WORDS ABOUT DOMAIN NAME AVAILABILITY

Because Web sites are one of the most important elements of a company's identity nowadays, your choice of a Web site address (URL) is increasingly important. To determine if your company (or product) name is available on the Web, visit *www.whois.com*. At this site, you can type in the Web site address you want and see if it's available.

If the name is already in use, don't get discouraged. These days, more than *one million* dot-com domains are created daily. If someone else has your dot-com domain name, other options include:

- Use the same domain with a different extension. Dot-net (.net) and dot-biz (.biz) are alternative ways of obtaining the domain name you want.
- Dot-us (.us) is for American Web sites and is the newest extension. As of this writing, it has the largest number of available names in inventory.
- Purchase the name from another business. When you type in the domain name you're searching for at Whois.com, and it's taken, Whois.com will tell you who owns the name. You could track down the owner and make him an offer.

Because of the importance of Web sites in this day and age, it makes sense to make the URL search process an integral part of your name-generation process.

LIPE'S LAW OF NAMING

A good name (for either a company or a product) must pass the telephone test. Simply telephone five different people and say, "My company name is _____." If they:

- say "huh,"
- ask you to spell it, or
- say *"Gesundheit,"*

then reconsider your choice.

WHERE TO CHECK ON THE AVAILABILITY OF NAMES

The last thing you want to do is launch a new company (or a newly rebranded one) only to find that your company name is already in use. To avoid this, make your first stop the Secretary of State's Web site for your state. Many of these Web sites include a "Business Name Availability" search service that allows you to plug in company names and see if they're already in use.

To find your Secretary of State's office, type "business name availability [your state]" into a search engine and you should see your listing.

HOW TO PROTECT YOUR NAME

Once you've decided on a name, and found that it's available, how do you protect its use? A number of steps are available to protect it, but which ones you take depend on the type of business you run, whether your Internet site conducts commerce, and, most especially, the geographic scope of your business's physical assets.

If, for example, your business is strictly local (e.g., Aldrich Street Cleaners), then you'll want to register the name with the Secretary of State's office in your state by filling out a form and submitting a fee (somewhere in the neighborhood of $50).

I'd also recommend publishing your company name quickly after you receive confirmation from the Secretary of State's office. This helps you gain visibility;

more important, it establishes a permanent record of "first use" for the name. Immediately after receiving confirmation of my company name, I published an announcement declaring my business's formation in two consecutive issues of a local legal journal. This proved important eight years later when my company was involved in a trademark dispute.

If your business is a corporation, many states require you to include such words as *corporation, company, incorporated,* or *limited* in your name. Read the fine print closely when filling out the forms from the Secretary of State.

DOING BUSINESS IN OTHER STATES

If your trading area includes other states, you'll probably want to register your name in those states as well. You can do this by writing the Secretary of State's office in those states and requesting the forms. I'm told you can register in all 50 states through the mail.

TRADEMARKS

According to the dictionary, a trademark is "any word, name, symbol, or device, or any combination thereof, used by a person, or which a person has a bona fide intention to use in commerce, to identify and distinguish his or her goods including a unique product from those manufactured or sold by others and to indicate the source of the goods, even if the source is unknown." Trademarks can be registered in individual states or at the federal level through the U.S. Patent and Trademark Office (USPTO). For more information, visit *www.uspto.gov.*

Why would you seek a trademark?

- If you anticipate expanding into new markets, a trademark affords you protection to do this.
- If you want to erect a barrier to entry for your competitors.
- If you want to battle competitors who are importing knockoff versions of your product.

Trademark laws are complex, so if you're thinking of getting a trademark, consult with a trademark lawyer.

THE TOP REASONS TO CHANGE YOUR COMPANY NAME

In certain instances, a company should change its name. Although some of these examples are more drastic than others, the bottom line is that any of these situations signals it's time for a change:

When Your Products Outgrow Your Name

Let's say you start your company with the name Johnson's Welding Supply. Business hums along, and soon the company expands into welding services—for example, contract welding services and welding equipment repairs. As demand for these services grows, you find that your company's original name is limiting.

Companies like these have to change their names to account for their new mix of services. A more forward-thinking solution would be to avoid this situation altogether by initially crafting a company name that is broad enough to accommodate a shift in its core business. For example, this welding company could have been named Johnson's Welding World to leave room for future growth.

When Your Name Signals a Limiting Geographic Scope

Eckerd Drugs of Florida soon came to outgrow its name's geographic limitations and renamed itself Eckerd Corporation. Allegheny Airlines changed its name to US Airways Group, Inc., when surveys of travelers showed that 25 percent of them perceived it to be a regional carrier because of its name. At the time, it was the *sixth largest* passenger airline in the United States.

Any company that is naming (or renaming) itself should shoot for the broadest geographic reach possible with its name.

When Your Name Blends In with Others

There's nothing worse than blending in (the opposite of standing out). In the Minneapolis area alone, more than 70 companies have names that begin with the prefix "techn," including Techna, Techne, Technix, Techno, TechNoL, and Technomics. Be different: stand out.

Naming from a Fifth Grade Perspective

When my son was in the fifth grade, his middle school underwent a rebranding effort, and the fallout was significant. At the time, the school's mascot was a panther. Sleek, swift, and dangerous were the undertones, and I never heard one student complain. Then a few parents got it into their heads that a panther sent the wrong signal (I can only imagine why) and changed the mascot to the fish. Overnight, my son's school identity went from the panthers to the fish.

Call me a competitive, ex-jock, frat boy if you will, but this new identity sucks. How can anyone get excited about being a fish? What kind of imagery does this evoke? Even at the middle-school level, this new identity defines the students' collective personality. How do I know? Because when I asked my son how he felt about the whole thing, he looked at me, head in his hand, and mumbled, "We're just a bunch of fish now."

CHAPTER WRAP

The author Katherine Paterson once said, "The name we give to something shapes our attitude toward it." For this very reason, give your company name great consideration. It will figure prominently in every aspect of your company's marketing effort. Most times, it will form a critical first impression for your company. My hope is that it will form a good many favorable impressions after that.

14

TAGLINES

One of the Cheapest (And Most Effective) Marketing Tools

An idea is a point of departure and no more.
As soon as you elaborate it, it becomes transformed by thought.

PABLO PICASSO

I'm a big believer in taglines. In ten words or less, a strong tagline reinforces the very essence of your company's identity and hammers it home to buyers. Larger companies caught the fever for taglines a long time ago, but smaller companies will also find them to be the most efficient marketing weapons in their arsenal.

Simply defined, a tagline is a memorable phrase that sums up the core promise of a company's brand. Good taglines capture the benefits of doing business with your company, and exceptional ones embrace the emotions that your buyers feel. Good taglines are subtle; great ones are direct. In the end you want buyers, after reading your tagline, to say to themselves, "Oh, I get it."

Because your tagline is most often visually linked to your company name, it will also be one of the most visible facets of your company brand. Because your company's business cards, letterhead, Web site, brochures, flyers, newsletters, direct-mail pieces, trade show booth, and hundreds of other tools will carry your logo, they should also carry your tagline.

A great tagline will enhance your company's word-of-mouth. If you have a catchy or memorable tagline, you'll find that customers, vendors, and champions of your company may repeat it (or parts of it) as a way to better describe your company to others. Imagine the effect on your company identity when a customer, in response to a question about your company, responds by saying, "Oh, my insurance is with Allstate. You know—the good hands people." So help spread the word about your company by developing a catchy tagline that is easily remembered, and repeated.

FIGURE 14.1 *Popular Taglines from Hollywood*

Hollywood is especially good at developing taglines. Here are a few movie taglines you might remember:

Movie	Tagline
Star Wars	A long time ago in a galaxy far, far away . . .
The Empire Strikes Back	The adventure continues . . .
Rocky	His whole life was a million-to-one shot.
Apollo 13	Houston, we have a problem.
Wayne's World	You'll laugh. You'll cry. You'll hurl.
Platoon	The first casualty of war is innocence.
Who Framed Roger Rabbit	It's the story of a man, a woman, and a rabbit in a triangle of trouble.
When Harry Met Sally	Can two friends sleep together and still love each other in the morning?
Jaws	Don't go in the water.
Jaws 2	Just when you thought it was safe to go back in the water . . .
Monty Python and the Holy Grail	And now! At last! Another film completely different from some of the other films which aren't quite the same as this one is.
Groundhog Day	He's having the worst day of his life . . . over and over . . .
Poltergeist	They're here . . .
Poltergeist II	They're back . . .

Now see if you can guess which movies each of these taglines comes from:

a. In space no one can hear you scream.
b. This is Benjamin. He's a little worried about his future.
c. Nothing on earth could come between them.
d. The snobs against the slobs.
e. Same planet. New scum.

a. *Alien* b. *The Graduate* c. *Titanic* d. *Caddyshack* e. *Men in Black II*

SOME HELPFUL HINTS ON TAGLINES

Keep Them Short

The best taglines are short and to the point. Remember, if you want something to be remembered and repeated, it's got to be brief. Try to keep your company's tagline under ten words and you'll dramatically increase its recall value. Here are some examples of taglines that are short and to the point:

- *Just do it!* (Nike)
- *Like a rock . . .* (Chevy Trucks)
- *It's the real thing!* (Coca-Cola)
- *Quality is job one.* (Ford)

For taglines, keep them snappy and you'll be happy.

Single Out a Benefit

Another way to get your tagline remembered is to center it around a key benefit that your company provides. Some benefit-oriented taglines include:

- *You're in good hands with Allstate* (Allstate Insurance)
- *Fly the friendly skies* (United Airlines)
- *Like a good neighbor, State Farm is there* (State Farm Insurance)
- *The quicker-picker-upper* (Bounty)
- *Melts in your mouth, not in your hand* (M&Ms)

A Tagline Should Sync with Your Company Positioning

One reason Avis's *We try harder* tagline is so popular is because it reinforces the company's number 2 position behind Hertz. Realizing that it couldn't replace Hertz in buyers' minds, Avis instead positioned itself opposite the leader, proudly celebrating its number 2 position. This position painted Avis as the underdog, the little guy. Because so many people in this world root for the underdog, Avis's *We try harder* tagline not only was dead on with the reality of the situation, but it became one of the world's most memorable taglines.

STEPS TO DEVELOP A TAGLINE

Step #1—Find Your Word(s)

Begin developing your company's tagline by brainstorming all the words that fit tightly with your company identity. Ask your company's key executives (or your dog and cat if you're a freelancer) to come up with a list of words that your company stands for.

Even better, ask your customers to try boiling down the essence of your company into a *single word*. Use a mail survey, an e-mail survey, a company blog, warranty cards, short phone calls, or any other feedback mechanism you can think of to ask your customers what *one word* they'd use to describe your company. From these efforts, compile a master list of the best 25 or 30 words that are used by others to characterize your company, and then move on to the next step.

Step #2—Whittle Down the List

After generating your initial list, the hard work begins, for you'll need to narrow the list to just five words. For starters, eliminate words such as *high quality, service-oriented,* or *good value*. Although these words may aptly describe your company, they're just too general or vague to distinguish your company. Also remove any duplicate words. For example, if one of your spot-on words is *dependability,* then eliminate *reliable* and *trustworthy* because they're just other ways of saying the same thing. To get to your list of five spot-on words, examine each one on your list very carefully for its nuances, then eliminate the duplicates.

Step #3—Craft Phrases from Your Spot-on Words

After whittling your list to the five spot-on words, it's time to put on your copywriting hat. The goal for this step is to develop some creative phrases (remember, ten words or less) that incorporate these words. Here are two proven approaches you can use to develop a series of possible taglines:

Approach #1—The straight-ahead approach. Using this approach, you fill in the blanks to the following questions:

1. Our expertise is in _____ [your field].
2. What we offer our customers are _____ [your products or product category].
3. We appeal best to _____ [your target audience].

Let's say your answers to the three questions were:

1. Payroll
2. Software products
3. HR professionals

Now take these answers and insert them into this sentence:

XYZ Company—_____ _____ for _____.
                   [Field]   [Products]   [Target Audience]

Your working tagline, using this method, would be:

XYZ Company—Payroll Software Products for Professionals

This straightforward approach will generate a passable tagline. But something is missing. Can you guess what it is? A benefit. To develop a tagline that includes a benefit, move on to the next approach.

Approach #2—The bracket approach. Another way to generate a working tagline is to complete the following sentence:

_____

[Company name]
is the

_____

[Category]
that

_____

[Benefit]

With this approach, your tagline will better communicate the end benefit customers get when working with your company. Using this approach, a sample tagline might look like this:

XYZ is the payroll software company that gets employees paid on time.

GET HELP SMOOTHING THE EDGES

After using either of these two approaches, you'll end up with several working taglines. I suggest taking your working tagline(s) to a professional copywriter. In an hour or two (if she is any good), she will transform this working tagline into a more professional and many times more creative tagline that carries some zing. Don't overlook this important step in the process. Spending just a couple hundred bucks could impact your sales to the tune of hundreds of thousands of dollars. Remember, if you want your company identity to stand out, you've got to take some risks. To me, this is a gamble that could pay off big in the future.

ONE TRICK TO GETTING YOUR
TAGLINE REMEMBERED

The Web site *www.adslogans.com* once surveyed its visitors about advertising slogans. The survey looked at two variables:

1. Consumer awareness of popular advertising taglines and
2. How well these taglines were associated with the particular brands

The top three brand taglines in the survey (measured by the percentage of people who had ever heard them) were:

Tagline	Brand	% heard of
You're in good hands with _____.	Allstate	97%
Like a good neighbor _____ is there.	State Farm	92%
_____ gets the red out.	Visine	82%

Note: The actual company or product name was omitted when testing consumers.

What's significant is that each of these three leading taglines *includes the company name.* I think there's a lesson here: for maximum effect, see if you can't include your company name in your tagline.

TEST YOUR TAGLINE OUT

I know I sound like a broken record, but every aspect of your marketing should be tested, including your tagline. Take your top three tagline options and run them past your customers and suppliers. Which one(s) are they drawn to? Do any of them cause confusion? Which taglines light up their faces? Which ones furl their brows? As a general rule, the opinions you get from people outside your company should outweigh those from people inside the company.

If your company has a significant number of international customers, seek input from customers in these countries as well. The annals of marketing history are littered with examples of taglines that played well in the host country but created problems in other countries. For instance, when Burger King opened its first store in Australia, the company used a sign that said "Home of the Whopper" at a trade show. Little did they know that in Australia, a "whopper" is slang for passed gas.

ATTACH YOUR TAGLINE TO YOUR LOGO

Once you've developed a winning tagline, as a standard practice, always make it appear alongside (or below) your logo. This way, the buyer drinks in both a visual element (your logo) and a copy element (your tagline) at the same time. Pictures and words that go hand in hand almost always present the most powerful learning aids.

A TAGLINE AS A WEB SITE DEVICE

In Jakob Nielsen's book *Home Page Usability,* he writes:

Home pages are the most valuable real estate in the world. Millions of dollars are funneled through a space that's not even a square foot in size. The home page is also your company's face to the world. Potential customers look at your company's online presence before doing any business with you. Complexity or confusion make people go away.

Because of this, Nielsen feels that almost every Web site should incorporate a tagline. Given the value of this real estate, and the itchy mouse fingers most Web site visitors have, you have just seconds to capture a visitor's attention. Therefore, Nielsen argues, most Web sites should include a tagline that "emphasize[s] what your site does that's valuable from the user's point of view, as well as how you differ from key competitors."

LIPE'S LAW OF TAGLINES

Your company's tagline must differentiate you from your competitors. Collect three of your closest competitors' taglines and compare them to yours. If your tagline is interchangeable with the other ones, you still have work to do. Remember: a tagline should be *uniquely* yours.

CHAPTER WRAP

In today's market, your company has just seconds to capture a buyer's attention. Because a standout tagline can both catch the eye of your buyer *and* educate him about the value your company brings to his life, you should count on a tagline as an important anchor for your company identity.

15

LOGOS

Proven Techniques for Developing a
Unique Brand Mark

There is just no way any management with any intelligence and foresight cannot recognize the value of a corporate image. It is the best single marketable investment that a company can make.

MALCOLM FORBES, Founder of Forbes Magazine

During the 19th and early 20th centuries, a rancher would mark his cattle with a brand. This brand, which depicted an image unique to his ranch, helped to distinguish his cattle from another rancher's in the event of a broken fence.

Company logos, in today's marketing world, operate much the same way. A solidly designed logo can distinguish a company from its competitors by evoking certain images in a buyer's mind. And in today's cluttered market, where a buyer's attention may be diverted in just seconds, a good logo can be a positive trigger that reinforces the company's identity in the buyer's mind.

Without a strong logo to support your company's brand, your image may suffer from a lack of recognition or, worse, be perceived as less professional. Don't jeopardize your company identity with a poor logo, or no logo at all. Develop a standout logo that helps craft the right image for your company.

SHAPING YOUR BRAND IMAGE

Once you've decided to develop a company logo (or update your current one), try to first identify the actual personality of your company. Because your logo will visually represent this personality, it's important that you identify the exact brand image for your company. If you don't go through this step of identifying the brand image, you could make either of these two mistakes:

1. Presenting an inconsistent identity to your market
2. Handicapping any agency or graphic designer you bring in to help with your graphic design work

To prevent either of these from happening, follow these steps:

1. Identify Your Company's Adjectives

To accurately portray your brand image, you first have to describe it verbally using the right set of adjectives. Is your company sexy or sweet? Tough or tender? High energy or laid-back? Approachable or brusque? Caring or superefficient? Casual or corporate? Classic or contemporary? Funky or straitlaced?

Much like you did when developing your tagline, you'll need to brainstorm a list of ten or so adjectives that best describe your company's culture. If you have trouble with this, pick five outsiders and ask them this question: *If I asked you to describe our company's personality, what one adjective would you use?*

2. Equate It to a Person

After generating a list of adjectives, see if you can't name a famous celebrity whose personality comes closest to matching these qualities. Is your company personality closer to John Wayne or John Denver? Jimmy Stewart or Jimmy Kimmel? George Clooney or Wesley Snipes?

Is it more like Helen Hayes? Audrey Hepburn? Madonna? Lil' Kim? Shirley Temple? I like to use celebrities because their personalities are often universally known, so it's easier for a group of people to identify the celebrity who best exemplifies a company. After you've agreed on a personality, try to identify the characteristics that stand behind that celebrity. These are the adjectives then that describe your company personality.

If you're discussing your company's personality with an agency or designer, be sure you mention this celebrity. It's sure to spark a lively discussion about why you chose that person; more important, it will more clearly communicate the qualities and characteristics that stand at the root of your company's culture.

THINK THIS IS TOO TOUCHY-FEELY?

If you think this is all a bunch of hooey, ponder these questions: Do Marlboros really taste different from other cigarettes? Is AOL really better than Yahoo? Is H&R Block superior to the tax accountant down the street? No to all three.

These products are brand leaders because they've identified their company brands and painstakingly reinforced them over the years. Remember, a big reason customers choose to do business with a company is because they identify closely with that company's image. The core product or service may be of secondary importance.

Products are made in the factory, but brands are created in the mind.

WALTER LANDOR, Branding Visionary

FIVE REASONS YOUR COMPANY NEEDS A LOGO

1. A Logo Helps Buyers Identify with a Company

We, as people, make statements by the clothes we wear, the cars we drive, and the radio stations we listen to. In a business context, we also make statements by the vendors we choose, the services and products we buy, and the company we keep. So it should come as no surprise that many of us identify with certain companies directly through their logos. If you doubt this, the next time you're at a mall, take a look around and notice how many people are wearing company logos (e.g., on shirts, pants, hats, shoes).

2. A Logo Acts As a Reference Point

The right way to think about your marketing efforts is as a chain of events. First a buyer sees your ad in a trade magazine. From there, he visits your Web site. While at the site, he downloads your company's latest white paper. After reading the white paper, he decides to attend a Webinar that your company puts on. After the Webinar is over, he signs up for your free e-zine. And so the chain will continue until he buys.

At each one of these links in this chain of events, your logo is there to provide continuity. This ever-so-subtle form of constancy seeks to reassure the buyer, at each link in the chain, that he's still dealing with the same company—your company.

3. A Logo Can Be a Beacon in a Sea of Confusion

Now pretend that that same buyer is attending a crowded trade show where your company has a booth. As he walks down the bustling aisle, he's bombarded by stimuli. People shout out to him, inviting him over to their booths. Others thrust flyers and coupons into his hands. Signs leap out at him. Continuous-loop DVDs blare their messages. Our beleaguered attendee soldiers on, desperately trying to recognize somebody, something, anything.

Then, amidst this sea of confusion, he spots your logo on your trade show banner. And in that brief instant, he immediately recognizes your company and turns into your booth for relief. In this example, your company's logo has delivered an element of familiarity.

4. A Logo Distinguishes You from the Competition

Fast-forward six months and now imagine that this same buyer has requested proposals from your company and one other. As he sits in his office, pondering his final decision, he examines the two proposals in front of him. Your company's proposal cover features a distinctive four-color logo that portrays professionalism and confidence. The other company's proposal cover just has that company's name in 12-point Arial type. Which do you think the buyer is drawn to?

5. A Logo Can Grow into a Valuable Intellectual Property Asset

Repeatedly exposing your company's logo to millions of consumers adds value to a company's balance sheet—in the form of an intangible asset. Fortune 500 companies have realized this for years. But this lesson applies to small and midsize companies as well. If you ever plan on selling your company in the future, your logo can be yet another asset in the sale.

To be sure, businesses don't succeed or fail on the strength of their logos alone. But *not* having a first-class logo *can* sometimes raise a yellow flag in a buyer's mind, and plant a seed of doubt in her mind.

WINNING STYLES OF LOGOS

You (and your designer) can choose from several styles to develop your company's logo. They are:

1. Text Logos

This popular treatment stylizes the company name to produce a unique company logo. In Figure 15.1 is an example of a text logo for a client of mine, a leading provider of baggage carts, lockers, and strollers.

This is a very practical and workable approach if you want to draw special attention to your name. By using this approach, you will focus a buyer's attention directly on the company name itself, improving the chances it will be remembered.

2. Symbol Logos

Symbol logos incorporate an image that directly relates to the company's core attributes (i.e., name, benefits). Examples of this approach include the Red Cross logo, Apple Computer's apple, and the Traveler's umbrella. Figure 15.2 is an example from one of my clients, a leading distributor of mailing systems here in the Midwest.

FIGURE 15.1 *Text Logo*

Smarte Carte Inc.'s logo is straightforward and effective. The text logo style serves to distinguish between the two aspects of its name: smart and carts. Note that the logo carries the registered trademark symbol.

FIGURE 15.2 *Symbol Logo*

MN Mailing Solutions' logo incorporates an envelope graphic in motion. This effectively uses a symbol to further strengthen the company's identity as a leader in mailing systems. Note also that the tagline is prominently featured and carries a service mark.

One advantage to this approach is that many people's attention is initially drawn in by a graphic or visual. If you decide to use a symbol logo, make sure you keep its design simple. Some symbol logos involve complicated styling and this complexity may not translate well to different uses or sizes.

3. Stylized Lettering

You could also use a logo with stylized lettering to emphasize aspects of your company brand. In the example in Figure 15.3, for my company, the first two letters of the company name are stylized into a logo.

FIGURE 15.3 *Stylized Lettering Logo*

My company logo uses stylized lettering for the mark portion of the logo. This is also an example of a stacked logo that runs more vertical than horizontal. Note that the logo carries the registered trademark symbol.

4. Abstract Logos

An abstract logo also uses a symbol, but the image has no inherent tie to the company. A logo like this can unleash great brand strength because of its distinctiveness and it may be easier to protect.

Examples of well-known abstract logos are Nike's now ubiquitous "Swoosh" logo and Adidas's "Three Stripes" logo. Before you settle on an abstract logo, ask yourself if your company has the resources—both money and time—to make your logo a widely accepted brand mark.

LOGO DOS AND DON'TS

Here are a few dos and don'ts for developing your logo:

Dos

- *Do collect logo samples you like.* Find examples you like within your industry, but also look at logos in other industries as well. Many advertising firms and consumer goods companies sport creative logos, and by studying them, you'll draw a clearer picture of what you like and what you don't.
- *Do hire a designer.* Too many people learn a little PhotoShop, then see themselves as expert graphic designers. Don't fall into this trap. Highly regarded graphic designers have a lifetime of logo knowledge that's more expansive than yours. They also have access to more sophisticated software and images. Plus, they can help you understand how your logo will work across all your marketing media. Focus on your strengths and let your designer focus on hers.
- *Do envision all the uses for the logo.* Too often a logo is designed with just the business card or letterhead in mind. But if your company uses uniforms, premium items like golf balls, Web sites, or any of a thousand other vehicles, your logo must work there also. Remember, the best logo for your company will work well on *all* your marketing tools.
- *Do review designs with outsiders.* Relying solely on internal employees for feedback is dangerous. Bear in mind that the *real* audience for your company's logo are your buyers. Work hard to incorporate their opinions into the process using feedback sessions, online surveys, or focus groups.
- *Do get multiple versions of the final logo.* Because your logo will be used in a variety of mediums, it makes good sense to get multiple versions from your designer. At a bare minimum, insist on these versions:

— Small, medium, and large versions
— A Web version
— A print version
— A black-and-white version
— A color version

Don'ts

- *Don't forget to look at your graphic designer's logo.* When choosing a graphic designer, make sure you pay attention to her logo. The creativity she's poured into her *own* logo will give you an idea of how much she'll pour into yours.
- *Don't fall back on design clichés.* You want a logo that will help your company stand out, so make sure you (or your designer) don't revert to employing overused design conventions such as swooshes, globes, or arcs that surround the company name. Being original requires effort, but that effort *will* pay off in the end with a standout logo.
- *Don't forget to consider your company name in the design of your logo.* If your company name naturally carries imagery (i.e., Lightning Recovery Systems *or* Rainmaker Corporation), ensure your logo ties into this imagery.
- *Don't scrimp and save.* Your logo will be seen by more people than you can imagine. Now is *not* the time to turn to the college intern for help. Spend the time and money to do it right by working with an agency or graphic designer who knows what she's doing.
- *Don't abandon your current logo without a very good reason.* It takes years, sometimes generations, to build up the recognition in a company's brand. Changing your company's logo just because the marketing staff is bored with it can be a lot like changing horses in the middle of a stream.
- *Don't use clip art.* If you want originality in your company identity, you need original art, which makes a more impressive statement about your company identity and is more distinctive.

WAYS TO TEST YOUR LOGO

There's danger in just approving a newly designed logo without some kind of testing. Here are a few ways to test your new company logo to see if it's the right one for your company:

View the logo in various formats. View the logo in color and in black and white. Have the designer reproduce the logo in a 1" × 1" size (to replicate the logo in a directory listing) and also in a 1' × 1' size (as on a trade show booth banner).

View the logo in your existing materials. Cut out versions of the new logo and paste them into your more common marketing materials—brochures and flyers perhaps. This way, you can see what the logo looks like "in action."

Share it with others. When you have logo options, feel free to show them to trusted friends, family members, and advisors. If they don't welcome the logo design with open arms, ask them why. If they like what they see, delve deeper by asking them to describe the logo using only one word. This is one way to get more insightful comments than "It looks cool" or "I just like it." If the word they use to describe your logo matches up with keywords that support your company image, then your logo is on the right track.

View it up close and far away. The number one mistake I see companies make when designing a logo is not considering its range of uses. Too many marketers pick the winning logo in a conference room with artificial lights, looking at a sample that's six inches square. What they fail to realize is that this same logo must be visible hundreds of feet away.

I once enlarged a client's logo from four square inches to five square feet and mounted it on the outside of a building. I then drove by the building at 60 miles per hour to see how visible the logo would be. Why? Because the company was about to launch a billboard advertising campaign and I needed to know that the logo would register well with the drive-by audience.

TRADEMARKS: HOW TO PROTECT YOUR LOGO

Once you've decided on a logo, a good idea is to register it to prevent other companies from infringing on it. A *registered trademark* gives your business exclusive rights to use the logo and enables you to lawfully prevent any parties from using the same trademark in the future. Trademarks can also refer to product names (e.g., ABC® Stereo Loudspeakers).

If your company is American, you can apply for a trademark at the U.S. Patent and Trademark Office Web site at *www.uspto.gov/teas/index.html*. While there, just follow the links to "Apply for a NEW mark" and you can file the application online. Many states also have trademark registration laws, but the federal procedure provides the broadest protection.

Most Common Logo Placements Checklist

Here is a checklist of some of the more common vehicles that will use your new logo:

- ❏ Business cards
- ❏ Letterhead and envelopes
- ❏ Wearables—(i.e., T-shirts, hats, coats)
- ❏ Premiums—(i.e., coffee mugs, golf balls)
- ❏ Annual reports
- ❏ Promotional brochures
- ❏ Advertisements
- ❏ Packaging
- ❏ All company signage including directional signs ("All deliveries this way . . .")
- ❏ Storefronts and store interiors
- ❏ Reception area signage
- ❏ Conference rooms and boardrooms
- ❏ Web sites
- ❏ Business vehicles (sales, service, delivery)
- ❏ Uniforms
- ❏ Trade show booths and banners
- ❏ Your building's exterior appearance
- ❏ Coupons
- ❏ Warranty cards
- ❏ Point-of-purchase materials
- ❏ Maps
- ❏ Directories

For trademark registration in foreign countries, consult the relevant agency in that country about the proper procedures to follow.

What Is a Service Mark?

A *service mark* is similar to a trademark, but it is used to identify and distinguish the services of one company from another. Like a trademark, it is denoted by the notation ^{SM} prior to registration (like ^{TM} for a trademark) and by $^®$ once registered. Service marks typically refer to services (e.g., XYZ$^®$ Payroll Services) and taglines.

What Do ^{TM}, ^{SM} and $^®$ Mean and When Should I Use Each?

A company displays the trademark designation ^{TM} next to a trademark that has not yet been registered. A company uses the service mark designation ^{SM} next to a service mark that has not yet been registered. Companies may only use the federal registration symbol $^®$ once a trademark or a service mark is actually registered in the U.S. Patent and Trademark Office. This symbol informs other companies that you have the right to take legal action if the trademark or service mark is infringed on by another.

The federal registration symbol $^®$ provides the following benefits:

- It demonstrates ownership of the trademark.
- It grants exclusive rights to use the mark in connection with the goods and/ or services noted in the registration.
- It can be used as a basis for obtaining registration in foreign countries.
- It can be filed with U.S. Customs Service to prevent importation of infringing foreign goods.

Finally, before heading too far down this path, it would be wise for you to consult with a qualified intellectual property lawyer or read the information found at the U.S. Patent and Trademark Office site located at *www.uspto.gov.*

PUBLISH SOME GUIDELINES

To ensure the consistent use of your logo throughout your company, you should develop a standards manual—also called a stylebook or style manual. I'm *not* talking about a humongous book that doubles as a weight training device. The best logo standard manuals are simple (just like the logo, right?) and give detailed guidelines for your logos:

- Size
- Colors
- Fonts (sizes and styles)
- Tints
- Minimum clear space around the logo

- Locations or placements on the page
- Reproduction (e.g., always reproduce from original art)
- Sub-branding
- Tagline usage

A stylebook simply can be a three-ring binder with examples of how you want your logo to appear. This is a great resource for external suppliers who may help you develop company identity materials. It can also act as an internal training device for any employees who work with the company logo.

LIPE'S LAW OF LOGOS

If someone has to spend more than five seconds figuring out what your logo represents, go back to the drawing board. At that point, it's safe to say that your logo is making people work too hard.

CHAPTER WRAP

In my opinion, every company in the world today should have a logo. A really good logo crafts a visual identity and adds an air of professionalism. As a result, a logo can be one of the best investments you'll make in your company brand. With a logo paired to a catchy tagline (discussed in the previous chapter), you'll offer buyers the right pictures and words to reinforce your company's image.

16

HOW TO USE COLOR TO REINFORCE YOUR COMPANY IDENTITY

Form follows function–that has been misunderstood.
Form and function should be one, joined in a spiritual union.

FRANK LLOYD WRIGHT

How do you feel when you walk into a pink room? What's your first reaction when you see a red street sign? What's your first thought when you see someone dressed entirely in black? Since early childhood, color has triggered in each of us a wide range of emotions, so much so that we often take color for granted. Don't. The success of your company's identity program hinges on the proper use of color.

Often referred to as the "silent salesperson," color can attract a buyer's eye, plant feelings in her heart, and draw her into your message. Over time the buyer will associate certain colors with your company, and will instantly recognize any communication of yours—as long as your company's colors are used consistently.

Face it, good use of color can sear your company's identity in a buyer's mind. Bad use will get you remembered for all the wrong reasons. So let's take a walk down the yellow brick road of color (or is it bisque, saffron, or tawny?).

COLOR 101

Any discussion of color has to begin where we left off in grammar school art class. There we learned about the three types of colors—primary, secondary, and tertiary. *Primary colors* are considered the foundation of color because, when mixed together and in different combinations, all other colors are created from them. There are just three primary colors—red, yellow, and blue. Take a close look at toys, children's books, and children's Web sites, and you'll notice that they contain blocks of bright primary colors. This is because young children respond more positively to primary colors than to pastels or muted blends.

Secondary colors are formed by mixing equal amounts of primary colors and include orange (red and yellow), green (yellow and blue), and purple (red and blue). Primary and secondary colors are used in company identity work to attract attention and create energy.

Tertiary colors make up the remaining color tones. Because they come from various mixtures of primary and secondary colors, they number in the millions and are used in a multitude of ways.

RED

Red grabs our attention. Because it's the warmest and most energetic color in the spectrum, red is a color that can literally turn us on. People surrounded by red may find their hearts beating faster. Not surprisingly, the ancient Romans waved a red flag as a signal for battle.

Because it carries a jolt of energy, red should be used lightly to help create your company identity. Use it to call out sections of copy in a direct-mail piece or a burst on your Web site, or to highlight your warranty in a brochure sidebar. Red draws the buyer's eye and can be used very effectively to highlight important communications—just don't overuse it.

When red tones are deepened to shades of burgundy, a consumer may respond to these wine tones as rich, refined, and expensive. For an example of this, check out Marriott.com *(www.marriott.com).*

Major brands using red: Coca-Cola, Budweiser, Avis, Dow, Marriott, Xerox

BLUE

Ask any group of people what their favorite color is and a clear majority will say blue. Over the ages, blue has become associated with steadfastness, dependability, and authority. It shouldn't surprise you to know that in ancient Rome, public servants wore blue. Look around you today and notice how many uniforms—police and other public servants—are blue. It should come as no surprise that the helmets for United Nations' soldiers are blue.

Research has also shown that seeing the color blue causes the body to produce chemicals that are calming, thus slowing the pulse rate. As a result, think of blue as a color to ease jangled nerves.

Major brands using blue: Tiffany & Co., Fairfield Inn by Marriott, Candlewood Suites

YELLOW

Yellow reminds us of sunshine, light, and warmth. Be careful not to overuse the color, though; yellow can quickly overpower someone if too much is featured. Instead, use yellow as an accent to call attention to something. In nature, yellow and black work well together to draw attention: think sunflowers and honeybees.

Major brands using yellow: McDonald's, Hertz, Kodak, Caterpillar, GameWorks

GREEN

Green is the color of growth, nature, and money. Along with blue, green is another calming color. Green is most often associated with envy, good luck, generosity, and fertility. The dark forest green can create conservative, masculine, and wealthy feelings.

However, green does have some cultural stigmas attached to it. For instance, in China, a green hat means a man's wife is cheating on him. In France, studies have indicated green is not a good color choice for packaging.

Major brands using green: Lawn-Boy, Fujifilm, Greenpeace, Courtyard by Marriott, SnackWell's

ORANGE

Orange is seen as the warmest of all colors, and as a result is often associated with fun times, energy, and warmth. There is nothing even remotely calm about this color. Orange can be used sparingly as a highlight color, but it is not a good choice for conveying a serious message.

Lighter shades of orange, such as peach, apricot, coral, and melon, can be pleasing to the eye and seem to appeal more to the affluent market. Internationally, orange is popular in cultures such as Mexico and India.

Major brands using orange: FedEx (orange and purple)

PURPLE

When you think of royalty, what color comes to mind? Purple. Because the robes of kings and queens were purple, we often associate the color with wealth, prosperity, and rich sophistication. Use purple carefully to lend an air of mystery, wisdom, or respect. Because the color purple seldom appears in a natural setting, it can also be considered exotic. Caution: in Brazil, purple represents death.

Major brands using purple: FedEx (purple and orange)

BROWN

Brown conjures up images of reliability and stability. Because brown is the color of the earth (terra firma), it is often associated with natural or organic things. Caution: in India, it is the color of mourning.

Major brands using brown: UPS, Residence Inn by Marriott

BLACK

Black is the absence of light and therefore is a somber color that, many times, is associated with evil (e.g., the cowboy with the black hat). Black can also connote authority and power. In some countries, black is associated with sophistication and elegance (e.g., a black-tie event).

For more variety in your visuals, try using various "screens" of black. This is accomplished by varying the tinting of the color and can produce such shades as gray. If you have limited budgets, black can be a very versatile color once you start experimenting with it.

WHITE

For most of the world, white is associated with purity (wedding dresses) and cleanliness (doctors in white coats). White is also used to project neutrality or peace. In America, we use white in figures of speech like "lily white" and we commonly associate white with the good guy in movies.

Clean, pure, and simple, this heat-repelling color keeps you cool and invigorates your senses. In marketing circles, it is widely known that white is the best background color for Web sites. If you choose not to use white as the background color for your Web site, my advice is to test this very carefully.

A white flag is the universal symbol for truce; in China, however, white is the color of death.

COLORS THAT WORK TOGETHER . . . AND THOSE THAT DON'T

Based largely on the principles of the color wheel, Figure 16.1 contains a chart depicting color combinations that work well and those that don't. Remember that these are broad guidelines. Varying the tint or shade of certain colors may change the ways colors interact.

Use this chart for basic direction, then work with your designer to arrive at a color palette that works for your company.

FIGURE 16.1 *Color Chart*

Color	Works well with . . .	Doesn't work so well with . . .
Red	Brown	Green
Blue	Yellow	Orange
Yellow	Red, blue, green	Purple
Brown	Orange, yellow, other brown tints	Black
Green	Yellow	Red
Orange	Red, yellow, other orange tones	Blue
Purple	Black	Yellow
Black	Brown, silver, white, yellow	Orange (you'll forever be associated with Halloween!)
White	Black	Lighter tones of any color
Silver	Black	White

AVOID CULTURAL STIGMAS

If your company has an international presence, you'll want to know what stigmas are attached to your company color in the host country. For example, blue is a very popular color in the United States, yet in China it can be perceived as evil or sinister. Likewise, the color purple has gained a foothold in American culture (e.g., the movie *The Color Purple,* Prince's *Purple Rain* movie and album), yet certain shades of purple have always been associated with death and morbidity in Catholic Europe. If your company has international offices, you have an obligation to understand how certain colors are received in these countries.

USE THIS COLOR STRATEGY TO DIFFERENTIATE

Without a doubt, the best color strategy you can use is to *choose a color different from your competitors.* This sounds so simple, yet I see companies blunder here constantly. Don't choose a color that your competitor uses because buyers already associate that color with your competitor.

Instead, choose a color that's been ignored by your competitors. To help you identify what this color is, get copies of competitors' brochures, Web site pages, flyers, and any other marketing materials. Note which colors they already use in their logos, brochure headers and footers, signs, and their Web site's home page. If your competitors standardize their use of color at all, it will be in these areas. Then choose a color that you don't see represented here.

A NEED FOR CONTRAST

Contrast (when colors with opposing qualities are used together) is a key tool for marketers, especially when you want things to be read by your buyers. Look at this page for a moment. What do you see? Black type against a white background. This is one of the most basic contrasts available, and one of the most popular. The reason for this should be obvious: the black type contrasting against the white background produces the easiest type to read. When it comes time to discuss a layout with your graphic designer, argue for contrast.

How UPS Distinguishes Its Identity through Color

Have you seen how UPS uses its color as a focal point for its company identity? In advertising spots, the company's brown color is the primary color used, and even its tagline is *"What can brown do for you?"* If you visit the company's Web site, brown is featured in its logo, banner, subhead text, and textbox banners. And you've no doubt noticed that the company's uniforms also feature the color. Some of the company's other uses of the color include:

- UPS's 269 airplanes, affectionately called "Browntails," are painted brown.
- Every one of the company's 88,000 delivery cars, vans, trucks, and motorcycles are painted brown.
- More than 142,000 gallons of brown paint are used annually to keep the company's worldwide fleet painted.
- Approximately 1,673,000 yards of brown cloth and 175,000 miles of brown thread are tied up in its worldwide uniforms.

UPS exhibits a truly integrated use of color through all of its company identity efforts. And the company is so committed to the color brown that in 1998, it registered two trademarks for the color brown, thus preventing any other delivery company from using the color. Now that's a commitment to color!

Color Use in Book Covers

For my first book *The Marketing Toolkit for Growing Businesses,* I chose purple as the color for the cover because, after perusing shelf after shelf of business books, I didn't see one other marketing book using purple. Now, I'm surprised at how often I refer to my book by its color. For example, when I'm on the telephone with an editor or book reviewer, I often describe the book as "The one with the purple cover."

A HEADS UP FOR USING COLOR IN BODY COPY

According to Colin Wheildon's excellent book *Type & Layout: Are You Communicating or Just Making Pretty Shapes?*, comprehension decreases significantly when you use color types different than black. In a controlled experiment, he tested reading comprehension levels for five different colors of type: black, deep purple, French blue, olive green, and warm red. The result?

Reading comprehension was "good" for 70 percent of respondents when they read black type. Comprehension dropped to 51 percent with deep purple type, and none of the other three colors (French blue, olive green, and warm red) scored above 30 percent. Despite what the creative folks say, keep your type color black if you want your copy to be read and remembered.

SOME RULES OF THUMB ABOUT COLOR

1. Avoid using black text against a gray backdrop—it makes for difficult reading.
2. Use high-intensity colors (a pure hue with no other colors mixed in) to draw attention to something.
3. Colors found in nature are often less saturated and more pleasing to the eye than their artificial counterparts.
4. Avoid using white text on a black background (also called reversing) with large blocks of text. According to Wheildon, comprehension drops considerably.
5. Warm colors (e.g., red) can appear larger to the eye than cool colors (e.g., blue).
6. Screening colors (creating a lighter shade of a color) can create the effect of printing in multiple colors.
7. To darken any color, just add black.
8. The color of the paper you print on will affect the finished color of the ink.
9. Pantone Color Guides (*www.pantone.com*) are great tools to help standardize your use of color.

CHAPTER WRAP

When a men's athletic team sets foot in the University of Iowa's visitors' locker room, they are greeted by a very strange sight indeed. The entire locker room, including the urinals, is painted pink. Because pink has been shown to have a calming effect on humans, this school has decided to use color to its advantage.

LIPE'S LAW OF COLORS

When designing a logo that involves more than one color, always ask your graphic designer to show it to you in a black-and-white format. Some colors (for example, red and blue) look great together in color, but not in black and white. Always view black-and-white versions of color logos before finalizing any decision.

You as a marketer must also appreciate how influential color can be—indeed, to a buyer's behavior. Make wise decisions about color and you'll not only get your company noticed, but you'll also influence buyers' emotions.

17

BUSINESS CARDS, LETTERHEAD, AND ENVELOPES

Tips to Get the Most Out of These Fundamental Tools

It's better to be looked over than overlooked.

MAE WEST

Commonly called corporate identity materials, your company's business cards, letterhead, and envelopes are very important touchpoints for your business. Sure, they'll craft a first impression, but because these tools are often filed away in Rolodexes or file folders, they also create lasting impressions. Here are some tips for improving the quality of these key marketing tools.

BUSINESS CARDS

Design

- Your business cards must use the same graphics, colors, and typestyles as your other communications materials (letterhead, envelopes, brochures, Web site, etc.).

- If you live in the United States, limit your business card size to the standard size of 3.5" × 2". Anything bigger won't fit in your buyers' card holders. Business cards in Europe tend to be larger, but so are their card holders.

- Limit the number of fonts on your business cards to two.

- Your logo should appear in the upper left-hand corner of the card. Eye movement studies show this to be the very first place the human eye travels when someone is handed a new piece of paper.

- Make sure that all the information on your card is printed in a typeface that's large enough to be easily readable. Think eight-point type or larger.

- Although you may have "digits" for your cell phone, fax, e-mail address, Web site address(es), pager, and others, be choosy about which information *must* appear on your card. Business cards with too much information can create digit overload in some people.

- Don't use a vertical format for your business card. Many designers sell this design idea as a way to stand out, but the truth is it annoys your buyers. Most buyers will store your card in a card holder that more easily accommodates horizontal format cards. As a result, vertical format cards will sit sideways in these card holders. Stay with the tried-and-true horizontal card format.

- Ensure the text on your business card is easy to read. Make sure there's high contrast between the background and the type. Using a light background (preferably white) with dark type (preferably black) works best.

- Be sure to include your tagline on your business card.

- If you have a retail location(s), consider putting a small map on the back of the card showing people how to get to your location(s). If you do this, always orient the map by pointing out which direction is north.

- If any of the information on your cards changes (i.e., you move, you change phone numbers, you update your logo), print new cards. An old card with scratched-out information does your company identity a disservice.

- Always include your Web site address (URL) on your cards. Web sites are so important these days, and buyers so often visit Web sites as a next step after receiving your business card that you should highlight the Web site address. Make it a separate color or a larger type size or put the address on the back of the card.

- If you are in a profession where relationship selling is important, it may be a good idea to include your picture on your card. Real estate brokers, salespeople, speakers, authors, entertainers, and just about anyone else in the personal services arena should consider doing this.

- If you belong to any special organizations, or you've won any special awards, list these on your card. They can be a quick way to provide instant credibility to your business.
- Use a professional designer to produce your business cards. The extra amount you pay will easily be returned to you with a more polished, consistent image.
- Use the back of your business card to promote some aspect of your business. I feature a picture of my first book *The Marketing Toolkit for Growing Businesses* on the back of my card, along with some information about how to buy it on Amazon.com.

Proofing and Printing Your Cards

- Triple-check all the contact information and digits on your card before sending it off to the printer. Avoid getting that queasy feeling in your stomach when you first receive your new cards . . . and notice a typo.
- Most business cards are printed on 100-lb. glossy professional white or off-white stock. This is generally the least expensive option.
- Choose your paper stock carefully. The stock you choose can say as much about your company as the graphics appearing on the card.
- When determining how many cards you should order from your printer, calculate first how many you think you will pass out over a year's time. Let's say you figure you'll pass out ten cards per week. Then your total for one year would be 520 cards (52 weeks x 10 per week). Many printers want you to order quantities of 5,000 or more. If you do this, realize that you're committing to a *nine-year supply* of business cards.

Guidelines for Using Business Cards

- Keep your business cards with you at all times. Keep an ample supply in your wallet or purse, briefcase, notebook, house, and office.
- Keep an extra supply of 20 cards in your car glove compartment.
- If yours is a small business, consider posting your business cards on bulletin boards at the following locations:

  - Supermarkets
  - Schools
  - Stores
  - Churches

  - Libraries
  - Hospitals
  - Coffee shops
  - Smaller shopping malls

  - Restaurants
  - Banks
  - Convenience stores
  - Colleges

- Some people recommend giving out several cards at one time. I only recommend doing this if you first ask the person "Can I give you an extra card?" Don't automatically assume that everyone wants two of your cards.

Creative Ways to Use Your Card

- Include a business card in every product you ship.
- Always include a business card in any correspondence you send. Almost 95 percent of those business cards may get pitched, but that remaining 5 percent may be all it takes to land your new customer of the year.
- You can use your business card as a name tag. Get a transparent plastic cover with a pin and attach it to your lapel.
- Use your business card as a name tag on your briefcase. This way, your business card may turn into a conversation piece at a meeting or during a plane ride.
- Use your business card as an ad: many publications offer business-card-size classified ads. If you design your business card properly, it can double up as an ad in those publications.
- Print an offer on the back of your business card. One convenience store owner in West Virginia passed out 200 business cards to people she didn't recognize as customers and wrote on the back of the card that they were entitled to a free soft drink or coffee. Of the 200 cards she handed out, 51 were redeemed in her store. That's a 25.5 percent response rate.
- Consider printing helpful information on the back of your card. For example, you could print:

  - Home mortgage loan interest rates
  - Metric conversion tables
  - A chart that calculates 15 percent and 20 percent tips

  - A calorie table
  - A local sports team's schedule
  - Postal information
  - International monetary conversion tables

- Consider creating a business card in magnet form. Magnets are widely used to hold important papers on the refrigerator door at home and on file cabinets at work.
- If you do use a trademark or service mark on your card, make sure you use the proper symbol (™, SM, ®).
- If you're ever looking for a job, consider printing a portion of your résumé on the back of your card. Include skills, qualifications, and anything else pertinent to the job you seek.

Tips on Exchanging Your Business Card with Others

- Don't give out your business card too quickly. It may be perceived as pushy. Try to establish a conversation with your prospect first. Then say, as you're handing the person your card, "Here's a card of mine" or "It might make sense for us to exchange cards."

- Follow the lead of people from the Far East who tend to hand out business cards using both hands. It gives the impression that your business card is something very important.

- When receiving somebody else's business card, don't put it away or off to the side immediately. Instead, keep it in your hand for a while as you talk to your prospect, or place it on the table right in front of you as you continue the conversation.

- If somebody gives you his business card, you should give him yours in return.

- If you regularly do business internationally, consider using the back of your card to print a translated version of your business card in your buyer's language. A special touch like this will make a favorable first impression.

Business Card Information Checklist

Here's a list of all the possible information that could appear on your business cards. But remember, include only that information that is necessary.

Person
- Name
- (Nickname)
- Title
- Affiliations
- Professional/academic designations

Place
- Department/division name
- Organization street address
- Floor/suite/mail stop
- Alternate PO box address

- City/state/state abbreviation
- Zip+four/postal code
- Country
- Home street address

Communication

- Voice telephone/extension number
- Toll-free telephone number
- Mobile telephone number
- Pager number
- Fax telephone number
- Home telephone number
- E-mail address
- Web site address

Details

- Office hours
- Time zone
- Appointment fill-in
- Map/directions

Orientation

- Name of organization
- Business description
- Product/service categories
- Resource information
- Special offer
- Invitation
- Illustration/photograph
- Organizational affiliations
- Sponsorships

LETTERHEAD

Tips

- Make sure you have adequate space to write between the header and footer of your letterhead. I once had letterhead printed up with an elaborate and very wide graphic in the header. But this used up a great deal of space that could have been used for writing.
- Keep the writing space (the space between your header and footer) blank. Using a watermark image here (an image that appears in the background of the letterhead) could overshadow the text of your letter if you fax or copy the piece of paper. If you're determined to use a watermark on your letterhead, make it very light.
- Try to find room to include the following information on your letterhead:
  — Company name
  — Tagline
  — Logo
  — Mailing address (if your business is international, include your country)
  — Telephone number
  — E-mail address
  — Web site address
  — Fax number
- Once again, your logo should appear in the upper left-hand corner of the letterhead.
- Choose your paper stock very carefully. A too-heavy stock will crease noticeably when you fold it and a too-light paper stock will mean your text or graphics will bleed through to the other side of the paper.
- Check paper stock samples with your printer before making your final choice. Printers have many samples that they can provide. Fold each sample piece of paper stock into thirds to simulate putting it into a number 10 envelope (the standard business envelope). It's amazing the differences you'll see in just folding different papers.
- Pick a paper stock that complements the design of your letterhead. If your letterhead was designed with a professional image in mind, don't spoil it by printing it on a cheap paper stock.
- If your letters have a tendency to be more than one page, consider developing a second-page letterhead. To keep it simple, a second-page letterhead should only contain your company logo and slogan. Caution: you'll now have

to maintain two separate inventories and you can expect to use about twice as many first page letterheads as second page ones.

- Use the appropriate trade or service mark symbols.

ENVELOPES

- Envelopes are typically referenced by numbers, such as number 9 or number 10. Following is a chart of some common envelope types used today.

Number	Width × Length
9	3⅞" × 8⅞"
10	4⅛" × 9½"
11	4½" × 10⅜"
12	4¾" × 11"

- Your logo, tagline, and return address should appear in the upper left-hand corner.
- If you're on a strict budget, use self-adhesive labels developed for your business that include your logo, tagline, and return address. That way, you can apply them to a wide variety of store-bought envelopes, bags, or boxes.

PRINT ALL CORPORATE MATERIALS AT THE SAME TIME

As a final word of advice, print all your corporate identity materials (business cards, letterhead, envelopes, and/or labels) at the same time. This ensures better color matching and a greater consistency for your company identity. You'll also save money by "gang-running" all materials at the same time.

CHAPTER WRAP

Professionally designed and executed, your corporate identity materials can catch a buyer's eye and draw him towards your company. The materials are really an ultimate form of confidence builder for your company. Don't shoot your entire company identity effort in the foot by cutting corners with these materials. You don't get a second chance to make a first impression.

18

BROCHURES

A Workhorse for Your Company Identity

Consumers build an image as birds build nests.
From the scraps and straws they chance upon.

JEREMY BULLMORE, Former Chairman of J. Walter Thompson Co. & WPP Group

A brochure is your company's James Brown—the hardest-working marketing tool in your kit. When you stop and think of all the ways a brochure is used these days, it makes you appreciate just how indispensable this tool is. A brochure can

- create awareness with brand-new buyers,
- educate prospects about your company and its offering,
- motivate buyers to take the next step in the buying process,
- maintain a presence for your company in a buyer's files,
- inform potential business partners (e.g., accountants, lawyers, bankers),
- educate intermediaries (e.g., dealers, distributors),
- train new employees, and
- give media the background information they require for a story.

From acting as a leave-behind after sales calls to a pass-out at trade shows to a download on your Web site, a brochure can act as your company's locomotive, the engine that pulls the rest of your marketing train along. If you are really serious about making your company stand out from the crowd with its brochure, keep reading.

HOW WILL WE USE IT? LET ME COUNT THE WAYS

If you're developing your company's first brochure, or even if you're just updating your current one, the first thing to establish is exactly how it will be used. For example, if you know that many brochures are handed out at your company's trade shows, and most of the recipients are just tire kickers, you probably wouldn't design your brochure to be a 16-page 6-color brochure with an embossed cover. This could chew through your marketing budget in a hurry. If your brochure will be primarily downloaded from your Web site, you wouldn't want to develop a graphics-intensive brochure that takes lots of time to download. By determining the exact ways your brochure will be used, you can avoid embarrassing losses of time, money, and reputation. Start by answering these questions:

- Will the brochure be sent through the mail to anyone who inquires about your company?
- Would it ever be sent to "cold" prospects?
- Will it be used as a sales aid during a sales call?
- Will it be used as a leave-behind after a sales call?
- Will it be passed out at trade shows?
- Will it be used at point of sale?
- Can it be used as a training device for new sales representatives? New employees?

I once designed a brochure for a client in the wood displays and subassemblies market. As part of my research, I asked the head estimator what he'd like to see in this brochure. He quickly answered that he'd like to see a sketch sheet as part of the brochure. The reason? This estimator could do a more accurate job of bidding on a project if he first received a sketch of the proposed job from a client.

Hearing this, we designed a simple sketch sheet, emblazoned with the company's logo and contact information, that could be inserted in every brochure packet. After adding this low-cost tool to the brochure, we noticed that more and more requests for bids came with accompanying sketches. As a result, the estimator could process more bids faster.

KNOW EXACTLY WHO WILL READ YOUR BROCHURE

After you determine all the uses for your company's brochure, identify exactly who will read it. Will it be consumers? Business-to-business buyers? The president of a small company? The CFO of a Fortune 500 company? Design engineers for a store fixture manufacturer? Men? Women? Both? Generation Xers? Empty nesters? Buying committees? Executives? Middle managers? Entry-level staff?

Once you know who the intended audiences are for your brochure, you'll better tailor its language to them. Here are some of the most common *primary readers* for any brochure:

- Prospects
- Customers
- Referral sources
- Sales and service representatives
- Employees
- Contractors
- Intermediaries
- Temporary workers

Remember Your Secondary Readers

Another group of influential readers might take an interest in your brochure: *secondary readers*. Although these folks may never buy a thing from you, they can still provide your business with all-important word of mouth. Secondary readers include:

- Vendors
- Suppliers
- Board members
- Current investors (e.g., banks, venture capitalists)
- New investors (e.g., banks, venture capitalists)
- Chambers of commerce
- Members of the media

SEEK TOUCHPOINT FEEDBACK

Your employees who have direct contact with your customers (e.g., salespeople, inbound telemarketers, franchisees, customer service representatives) can and should provide valuable input into the brochure's content *before* you start developing it. Too often, I see marketing departments jealously guard the task of developing a brochure, and refuse to involve others in the process. Yet, when they introduce the new brochure to the sales force, what do you suppose happens? The sales representatives, who now feel slighted by being ignored during the process, give the new brochure a hardy thumbs-down and refuse to use it.

From the get-go, seek input from those closest to your customer. You'll end up with a much higher-quality brochure *and* you'll motivate these key people to use it.

THE BASICS EVERY BROCHURE MUST COVER

Developing a new brochure can be a daunting task: include too much information and you'll bore your readers to tears; skimp on the details and you'll leave readers with too many unanswered questions. I've found that if your brochure can cover these five topics, it will provide enough information for your buyers to take the next step:

1. Identifying a Reader's Pain

One of the fastest ways to grab a reader's attention and draw that person in is to call out his or her pain. By using pain statements, which are phrased as either questions or statements, you'll get right to the heart of your buyers' frustrations. For example, a business-to-business travel agency could pose the question, "Does your business need to outsource its travel arranging and get back to doing what you do best?"

A company that sells lawn-care products to consumers could use the pain statement, "Are you sick of spending Sundays mowing the lawn? Wouldn't you rather watch the ball game?" Statements like these form an immediate bond with those readers who feel this same pain.

2. Benefit Statements

Follow up your pain statements with benefit statements that point out how your company (or product) makes a buyer's life easier. In Chapter 2, I listed the most common benefits that both business-to-business and business-to-consumer companies offer. Drawing on these, your benefit statements that would follow the previously mentioned pain statements might be:

- Pain statement: *Does your business need to outsource its travel arranging and get back to doing what you do best?*
- Benefits statement: *XYZ's outsourced travel program can free up your staff from the time-consuming chore of booking travel arrangements. With just one call, you can turn this task over to a qualified agent and refocus on the more important parts of your job.*
- Pain statement: *Are you sick of spending Sundays mowing the lawn? Wouldn't you rather watch the ball game?*
- Benefits statement: *With XYZ's breezy-pace mower, you'll have enough time to mow the entire lawn, trim the hedges, and drink a tall, cool one all before kickoff.*

3. Your Company's Uniqueness

Buyers want to know what makes your company superior to others. If your company uses a unique process, describe it. Does it possess an unusual piece of machinery? Cover it. Does your company boast a different set of clients? Talk about them and why they choose to do business with you.

The trick is to keep this section short yet enticing. If you do, the first conversation between a buyer and one of your sales representatives might just start with the buyer saying, "Tell me more about this unique part of your business you mention in your brochure."

4. Services (or Products) Offered

Some buyers want to see a broad range of services, and others are just looking for the one service they need. That's why I advise clients to list their five most popular services (or products) in a sidebar somewhere in their brochure. Any less than that and you'll look like a small-time player; any more and you'll look desperate.

5. Call to Action

This section, usually titled "Next steps" or "What to do next," is a vital part of any brochure, yet many companies forget to include it. Remember, one of your chief responsibilities as a marketer is to get your buyers to take the next step. If you don't provide explicit instructions to your buyers on how to do this, your brochure hasn't done its job. Here are some examples of motivating calls to action:

- *"So call 888-555-1212 today and learn how XYZ Company can make your life easier."*
- *"Visit* www.emergemarketing.com *and click on the link "Case Studies" to see how I've helped other companies just like yours."*
- *"Send us a check for $9 and start enjoying these insider resources today."*

Don't shortchange all the work and effort you've put into developing your brochure by leaving it up to the reader to take the next step. You've got to tell him how.

LIPE'S LAW OF BROCHURES

Always Provide Three Ways to Respond

In today's world, there are three types of buyers: hot, lukewarm, and just kickin' tires. To appeal to all of them, include three calls to action, one for each buyer:

- Call 800-555-1212 to speak to a sales representative (for the hot buyers).
- E-mail *tbd@yourcompanyname.com* with any questions you might have (for lukewarm buyers).
- Visit our Web site at *www.yourcompanyname.com* for more information (for just kickin' tires buyers).

STANDOUT SECRETS FOR YOUR BROCHURE

Up to this point, I've covered the mandatory parts of any brochure. Here are some additional elements you may wish to include:

A Cover Headline

Too many companies miss a great opportunity by just slapping their company name and logo on the brochure's front cover. Capitalize on this prime real estate by including a thought-provoking headline. For one of my clients in the printing business we included this headline on its brochure cover:

Does your printer offer you strategies and solutions?

This was important to call out because this core competency—offering proactive printing strategies and solutions—was a unique point of difference for my client.

Testimonials

Nothing beats having someone else sell your company. Testimonials are still one of the most effective ways to establish credibility with new buyers, and have others do the selling for you. In any brochure, I advise my clients to either sprinkle testimonials throughout or feature several of them together in a section called "What others say about XYZ Company." For more tips on how to get great testimonials for your business, turn to Chapter 12.

A Comparative Grid

As the title implies, this is a grid that directly compares your company to others. The grid lists your company, along with several competitors, down the left-hand side. Then, across the columns, it lists specific attributes of the service or product you provide. These could be a 30-day money-back guarantee, a 24-hour hotline, a five-year warranty coverage, or any others you can think of. Then, simply checkmark which attributes each of the companies possess. In an ideal grid, every attribute would be checked for your company while just a few are checked for your competitors. The lack of checkmarks in your competitor listings positions your company as superior in the minds of your buyers. A tool like this will also be warmly welcomed by your sales force because it can be used as a handy sales aid during a call.

WORLD'S WORST BROCHURE MISTAKES

I have a file folder full of awful brochures. From misspellings to pictures so dark they resemble ink blots, I affectionately call this my "Foul-Ups, Bloopers, and Blunders" file. Here are some of the most common brochure mistakes drawn from that file:

- *Leading off with your mission statement.* A mission statement is an internal tool that's used to generate focus for your business. In my opinion, it has no place in a company brochure because readers only want to know how your company is going to solve *their* problems. Save your mission statement for your boardroom walls.
- *Showing a picture of your building.* Most building shots look the same and do nothing to distinguish your company. Instead of showing the outside of your building, I recommend focusing on the problem-solving abilities *inside* your building.
- *Including instantly obsolete information.* Prices increase and staff depart. As a result, don't put either in your brochure. Instead, include this information on separate sheets that can be reprinted easily. Other things to avoid saying:
  — "We are ten years old"—instead say, "We've been in business since 1994."
  — "This year, we added 37 staff members"—next year, this statement will be obsolete.
- *Trying to close sales with a brochure.* Few brochures can guide a buyer all the way through the purchase process to a sale. Design your brochure so that it sparks a reader's interest, then provides information for further follow-up. Remember: *titillate, scintillate, then motivate.* That's all a brochure should do.

THE THREE BASIC BROCHURE STYLES

There are dozens of brochures styles to choose from, and any printer would be delighted to tell you about all of them. For now, I'd like you to consider just three different varieties. They are the:

- Trifold brochure
- Self-mailer
- Double-pocket folder brochure

No matter how big your company is, you can find the right brochure style for your company among these three.

The Trifold Brochure

To envision a trifold brochure, take a single sheet of 8½" × 11" paper and fold it into equal thirds. You will end up with a single sheet of paper that has six panels: three on one side and three on the other. Depending on how the paper has been folded, you will end up with either the z-fold or the barrel fold. Figure 18.1 shows how they both look.

Trifolds are ideal for companies with limited budgets. (See Figure 18.2 for the pros and cons of using the trifold brochure.) They also work well for companies that rely on point-of-purchase materials to sell their products at retail. One example we're all familiar with is the literature racks at tourist centers. A great many brochures found on these racks are trifolds. Also, if your company typically sends brochures through the mail to those who inquire (e.g., direct-mail companies), then a trifold would be a good choice.

FIGURE 18.1 *Trifold Brochure*

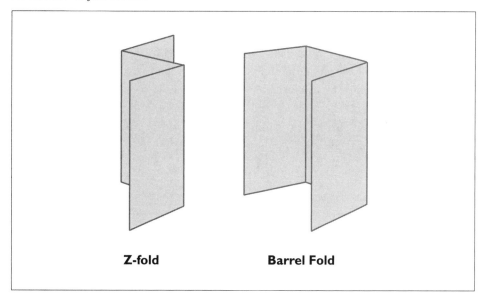

Z-fold   **Barrel Fold**

FIGURE 18.2 *Trifold Brochure Pros and Cons*

Pros	Cons
■ Is less expensive to produce. ■ Fits nicely in a standard envelope (number 10)—so it can be inserted in invoices, letters, or statements. ■ Copy is limited, so it may be easier to read. ■ One panel can be used as a tear-off reply card. ■ Easier to store inventory.	■ Information is static—adding new information usually means reprinting. ■ Has space limitations. ■ For a company brochure, this format may communicate "small business."

The Self-Mailer

This is a brochure that is designed to be put in the mail directly, without using an envelope. There are numerous formats for self-mailers, but the most common are:

- *Trifold self-mailer*—a trifold brochure in which one of the six panels carries the company's mailing address and any permit mailing graphics
- *Singlefold self-mailers*—usually folded into a finished piece that measures 8½" × 5½"

For any self-mailer, a recipient's address is applied to the mailing panel using either an inkjet printer or a mailing label. If your company markets its products or services directly to buyers, a self-mailer is ideal. Because it needn't be inserted in an outer envelope and the mailing address can be applied directly to the mailing panel, this is a terrific format for mailing to cold prospect lists. See Figure 18.3 for the pros and cons of using a self-mailer.

FIGURE 18.3 *Self-Mailer Pros and Cons*

Pros	Cons
■ Good for mailing to cold prospects. ■ Can mail to very large quantities. ■ Easier to store inventory.	■ Even less space is available than with a trifold because of the mailing panel. ■ Information is static—adding new information usually means reprinting. ■ Can be perceived as junk mail. ■ Not a good piece to mail to inquiries. ■ Not as versatile because of the mailing panel. ■ Must adhere to paper stock requirements because of postal regulations.

FIGURE 18.4 *Pocket Folder Brochure Pros and Cons*

Pros	Cons
■ Is more impressive. ■ Offers plenty of space. ■ Adding new elements (reprints, photographs, press releases) is easy.	■ Costs are higher. ■ Has greater storage space requirements. ■ May look too fancy. ■ Some assembly is required. ■ Envelopes are also needed if the piece will be mailed. ■ Can be expensive to mail.

The Double-Pocket Folder Brochure

As the name states, this is a folder with pockets on either side. With a brochure format like this, you can fill the pockets with a variety of inserts that match up with each buyer's unique needs. Plus, the pocket folder brochure allows your brochure to grow with your company's identity. Over time, you'll no doubt acquire press releases, article reprints, testimonial sheets, price lists, PowerPoint presentations, coupons, photographs, and dozens of other items you haven't yet imagined. A pocket folder brochure easily accommodates these new items. See Figure 18.4 for the pros and cons of using a pocket folder brochure.

SOME TIPS FOR MAKING YOUR BROCHURE SING

Back up any claims. Use statistics, new data, and metrics to support all your arguments.

Don't puff up. Overhyping ("the best widgets in the universe") smacks of amateurism. Stick to the facts and always back them up.

Avoid industry jargon. It won't impress your audience. In fact, it might just appear as if you're talking down to them. Abbreviations like AMA should always be introduced first with their full name and the abbreviation following (e.g., American Marketing Association (AMA)).

If you have room, consider adding a FAQ section. A frequently asked questions (FAQ) section indicates to your readers that you've thought through the issues they're grappling with. For advice about which questions to feature, check with your sales or customer service staff for the most commonly asked questions they receive.

Break up copy with subheads. Subheads are headlines that introduce new sections of copy; they are especially useful for breaking up long sections of copy. If your readers are anything like me, their reaction to looking at a solid block of copy is "Oh man, I'm not going to read *all that*." Subheads help readers skim your copy and emotionally prepare themselves for reading your brochure.

Use bullet points liberally. Another way to help today's busy buyer is by using bullet points to emphasize your more important points. Use them to highlight standout copy sections (e.g., benefits) and prevent eyestrain.

Commit this rhyme to memory:
If you want to sell Johnny Green
what Johnny Green buys,
You have to see Johnny Green
through Johnny Green's eyes.

Use power marketing words. Some words elicit more visceral reactions from people. Unfortunately, many are four-letter words. But marketing experts have discovered that certain words really pack a wallop. Here are 25 of the most powerful words known in marketing. Sprinkle them throughout your marketing materials and you'll *benefit* from better *results* and higher *sales* (that's three right there):

- You/your
- Free
- New
- Save
- Money
- Results
- Health
- Easy
- Proven
- Safe
- Guarantee
- Benefit
- How to
- Now
- Love
- Fun
- Finally
- Discount
- Special
- Breakthrough
- 100 percent
- Secret
- Last chance
- Unique
- Sales

If you're looking for more, check out the book *Words That Sell* by Richard Bayan. This handy book lists more than 2,500 high-powered words that will pack a punch for your brochure copy.

Use benefit-laden captions. If you show pictures, make sure each one is accompanied by a caption. And to get even more oomph from this short section of copy, try to call out a significant benefit that the picture subject offers. For example, a picture of me and one of my clients working together might have the caption: "Joe Client (right) and I are developing his company's first marketing plan. Joe's marketing plan has helped his sales force stay in front of its prospects and generate a steady stream of new leads." This goes past a straight narrative description of what's in the picture to reinforce one of the more important benefits clients get from working with me.

Occasionally, let some humor show through. Make them chuckle. It'll help break the ice and may be the nudge one of your buyers needs to pick up the telephone and call you.

HINTS ON PROOFING YOUR BROCHURE

A friend of mine, who once served in the army, always uses the expression "Check, check, and recheck." Applied to brochures, this means always proof your entire brochure *three times* before shipping it off to the printer. I'll bet you a dollar you'll find *at least* one additional error that third time around.

Send e-mails to all the e-mail addresses listed in your brochure. Visit any Web sites that are cited. Double-check the spelling of people's names. Make sure every photograph is assigned the right caption. No one wants to reprint a brand-new batch of brochures because one digit in a phone number was wrong.

Use print codes to stay organized

If you expect to reprint your brochure in the future, add a print code in the lower right-hand corner of the back cover. For most companies, this print code can be just the date of its printing (e.g., 12/06). When you reprint that brochure, change the code to reflect the new date. This coding system will come in handy when you get a call from one of your sales representatives who requests ten copies of "the brochure we got at the sales meeting three years ago." Just ask him to read the code to you on the back and you'll know which one he's talking about.

BEWARE OF GRINDING DOWN

I once worked with a company that spent entirely too much time developing its brochure. For every page of this brochure, we developed *three drafts* of copy, and agonized over every word of it. As a result, the process sucked the life out any creativity and ended up taking *twice* as long as it should have. Here's a sobering fact: buyers will only briefly glance at your brochure. Many won't read every single line of copy, so apportion your time accordingly. I'm not suggesting that you do a half-assed job; I'm just suggesting that you know when to move on.

KEEP ORDER QUANTITIES SMALL

Recently I talked with a client about updating some of his direct-marketing pieces. After I asked him when we could get started, his answer left a strange feeling in the pit of my stomach. "Not for a long time. We still have to work through the 5,000 postcards we bought three years ago," he said.

Beware the printer who says, "Why order 1,500 at $2 per piece, when you can order 5,000 at $0.90 per piece? You'll get a price break." Here are three good reasons not to fall for this:

1. If you do order 5,000 pieces at this price, your total price just increased 50 percent (1,500 copies × $2 = $3,000; 5,000 ×$0.90 = $4,500). Even though you pay a lower price per piece, you're still buying an additional 3,500, and spending $1,500 more.
2. You now have to find a place to stash 3,500 more pieces.
3. You lose flexibility to make future changes to your brochure. Let's say you print 5,000 new brochures, and six months later you want to change some copy (perhaps you've added a new product line or you changed your Web site address). Now you have to toss out your entire inventory. When you print your brochure (actually, this goes for *any* printed marketing piece), keep your order quantities low to start. You can always reorder.

THINGS TO DO ONCE YOUR BROCHURES
ARE PRINTED

- *Distribute them to every employee.* If yours is a small or midsize company, treat this moment as a teachable one. Send brochures to all your staff to reinforce the key points of your company identity.
- *Load a PDF version of the brochure onto your Web site.* According to *Internet Retailer* magazine, 73 percent of online consumers have looked at online versions of

brochures or flyers. Marketing is quickly becoming a self-serve industry. Load your brochure onto your site so others can help themselves to it.

- *Stash some copies for history's sake.* You may need them for legal reasons or to help you with some future, unforeseen project. I once did a positioning study for a Fortune 500 company and the company's old brochures were invaluable in helping me determine the path that the company had taken to arrive at its current positioning.
- *Consider sending copies to customers and champions.* Your new brochure, accompanied by a well-crafted cover letter, will oftentimes generate repeat business or referrals.

CHAPTER WRAP

Titillate, scintillate, and motivate. These are the three things any brochure must do to be successful for your company. Work hard to accomplish these three objectives, and your brochure will be the workhorse for your company identity efforts.

19

WEB SITES

Instant, Around-the-Clock, Around-the-World Tools

The road to success is always under construction.

LILY TOMLIN

Pretend for a few minutes that you're a prospective buyer for your own company. Let's say it's a Sunday night and you're lounging around in your pajamas watching television. Then it hits you that you have a staff meeting tomorrow and one of your employees will be reviewing the final two vendors that are bidding on the contract to install the new Accounts Payable software.

You're already familiar with one of the companies, but the other one is a bit of a mystery. To prepare for the meeting tomorrow, you decide to find out a little bit more about this mystery company. What would you do? If you're like the vast majority of people these days, you walk over to your computer and call up the company's Web site, and within 30 seconds you'd start forming impressions about the company as you surf its site.

This example underscores the power—the instant power—a Web site has on a company's identity. Within 30 seconds of deciding to learn more about your company, a buyer can do just that. Does your company's identity measure up to this instant scrutiny?

THE TOP TEN BENEFITS OF WEB SITES

If your company doesn't have a Web site, here are ten reasons to consider getting one—quickly:

10. *Generate more word of mouse.* According to Jupiter Research, 69 percent of consumers who receive a Web site recommendation from a friend pass it along to between two and six other friends. Word of mouth on the Internet (or word of mouse) is one of the most effective ways to generate awareness for a company.

9. *Generate more leads.* The most common complaint I hear among company owners these days is "We need more leads." What many of them fail to grasp is that an information-rich Web site that's professionally designed and easy to navigate will attract a host of new buyers to your company. Remember, too, that *not* having a Web site increasingly positions your company as behind the times.

8. *Qualify those leads.* As visitors navigate through your site, they are actually qualifying themselves. If they enter your "About Us" section, you know they are just getting acquainted with your company. If they sign up for your e-mail newsletter, you can assume they're interested in beginning a "platonic" business relationship with your company. Short of a personal sales call, where a dynamic dialogue takes place, you won't find another marketing tool this valuable for qualifying buyers.

7. *Attract new customers.* If you sell products on the Web, you'll learn over time that Web shoppers are a different breed from traditional retail shoppers. The online audience, by and large, is quite comfortable stopping by, introducing themselves, and purchasing your products without ever meeting you face-to-face.

6. *Offer a new way to purchase your products.* Pinched by the demands of more work and less time, most consumers turn to Web sites as time-saving devices. Buyers can learn more about your company, peruse your selection, and even buy something from you from the convenience of their own homes.

5. *Create anonymous shopping opportunities.* One great advantage to the Web is that it affords surfers the opportunity to page through your site and acquaint themselves with your company without ever divulging who they are. Increasingly, I find that buyers are reluctant to identify themselves to a company (and suffer a barrage of telemarketing calls from pesky salespeople), opting instead to remain on the proverbial sideline until they're ready. If you do a good (or even a passable) job of satisfying their needs in this anonymous stage, you can bet they will return and identify themselves when the time is right.

4. *Increase media access to your company.* A good Web site offers editors and reporters self-serve information on your company. Many of them are searching for experts or background information for pieces they are writing. Why not give them what they're looking for at your Web site? On a personal note, I once had a reporter download one of my articles and my biographical information from the "Press Kit" section of my Web site (*http://www.emergemarketing.com*). It was only when she e-mailed me, seeking my permission to reprint the article, that I became aware of her. The more accessible your Web site is to the media, the more your company will be written about.

3. *Transfer service functions to your site.* The U.S. Post Office now offers a value-added service called Delivery Confirmation. For around 50 cents, you can sign up for delivery confirmation on a package sent through the system. You track the progress of your package on the post office's Web site as it moves through the postal system. You can see when the package has reached its final destination and even who signed for it. This value-added service is extremely worthwhile for people who ship valuable packages.

2. *Hang sales tools off your site.* One of my larger clients hangs its latest Power-Point sales presentations off its Web site. That way, one of its sales representatives in Boston can give a product demonstration to a prospect in Wyoming without either of them leaving their offices. Think of the travel savings if you adopt this approach.

1. *Stay open 24 hours.* We all know how disappointing it is to drive to a store only to discover it's closed. These days, though, any company can be open for its customers 24/7—with a Web site. This is especially important if your company does business with overseas customers. Even though your employees are fast asleep, your visitors can still experience your company.

WHAT'S THE FIRST STEP TO DEVELOPING A WEB SITE?

If you're developing a Web site for the first time (or even if you're redesigning your current site), the success of the site will be judged on how well it achieves its objectives. So, do you have objectives for your Web site? To identify these, ask what you want your Web site to do:

- Achieve high search-engine rankings?
- Produce more leads?
- Generate additional subscribers?
- Sell advertising space?
- Sell more products?
- Generate income through affiliate links?
- Establish credibility?
- Increase your employee productivity?

After identifying exactly what you want to accomplish with your Web site, and prioritizing which tasks are most important, you will do a far better job of designing it.

THREE STEPS TO DESIGNING A SPOT-ON WEB SITE

According to *Internet Retailer* magazine, 50 percent of an online shopper's purchase decision is directly influenced by Web site design. So if your Web site's design isn't professional-looking, visitors won't stay around long enough to listen to what you have to say. Here are four easy steps you can take to design an effective Web site:

Step #1—Choose a visual identity for your Web site that syncs with your company identity. If you've already crafted a company image that emphasizes professionalism, then a Web site identity that's playful will furl more than a few brows. To craft a Web site image in keeping with its overall identity, a law firm might use subdued colors, serif typestyles, and copy with a serious and authoritative tone. If, on the other hand, your company appeals to a target audience of teenage girls, you'll want to use bright, bold colors, whimsical typestyles, and copy that has a fun, playful tone.

Step #2—Incorporate visual cues already being used off-line. If your off-line identity uses certain logos, visual elements, colors, and typestyles, try to incorporate these into your Web site identity. Picture a visitor to your site with one of your brochures in her left hand. Now imagine the reaction she'll have if she sees one identity reflected in her left hand and an entirely different one on her computer monitor.

Step #3—Draw visitors in with your first two paragraphs of copy. If visitors approve of your Web site design, the next challenge is to draw them in to learn more. The most effective way to do this is to pay close attention to the first two paragraphs of your Web site's copy–sometimes known as your opening statement. Based on studies, you've got between 15 and 30 seconds to convince a visitor to stay on your site, so the first 100 words of Web site copy have to be compelling.

Step #4—Work hard to make your site usable. Usability is the degree to which your site allows visitors to navigate your site and find what they're looking for. The field of Web site usability is getting more and more attention as the number of Web sites proliferates. For more information on this ever-evolving topic, read one of Jakob Nielsen's books (*Homepage Usability* or *Designing Web Usability*) or Steve Krug's book *Don't Make Me Think: A Common Sense Approach to Web Usability.*

IDENTIFY THE TOP THREE TASKS YOU WANT VISITORS TO DO

A short time ago, I was hired to audit a client's Web site. When I first spoke with the owner, I asked him to name the top three things he wanted visitors to do once they arrived at his Web site. He answered that he wanted them to:

1. Place an order for his products (a variety of spa covers).
2. Understand why his company's spa covers were better than all others.
3. Order accessory items.

Yet, when I visited his site the first time, I didn't see how I could do *any* of these three things. You must identify the most important things you want visitors to do, then design your Web site so these things are blindingly obvious to first-time visitors. Ask yourself, do you want your visitors to:

• Sign up for your e-newsletter?
• Purchase a product?
• Listen to a recording?
• Read a free article?
• Enter a password-protected area?
• Bookmark the site?
• Pass the site along to a friend?

Whatever your top three tasks are, work hard to make them highly visible on your home page. Box them in, shade them with a color, put them in bursts, or denote them with large button icons. Use whatever design ideas you and your Web site designers can come up with, but just don't leave them for visitors to discover by chance.

SUREFIRE WAYS TO BOTCH YOUR WEB SITE

Make the Average Download Times Exceed Ten Seconds

Let's say you've just opened an attractive new retail store. It's stocked with the classiest merchandise and staffed by helpful, eager salespeople. Yet, you allow customers to enter only *through the second-floor window*. Will it succeed? Of course not. You're making it too hard for the customer to enter the store. Yet far too many Web sites greet their visitors with huge graphic files or Flash animation on their home pages. Because many people still use dial-up connections (and have a decided lack of time on their hands), it's foolish to presume they will stay around for very long.

Put Up the Site, Then Leave It Alone

When I worked at a pharmacy during high school, the owner made us dust shelves and tidy up merchandise. Being a know-it-all youth, I thought this stuff was boring and didn't see how it would benefit a business. Now that I'm older, I see that I was wrong. Maintaining a store's interior provides the visitor with a more pleasant experience. The same holds true for a Web site.

Load new content. Update copy sections. Freshen up the graphics every so often. The aim is to lure the infrequent visitor back for another peek. And that won't happen with dusty shelves.

Hide Your "Pearls" Deep Within

Visitors to your site, especially new ones, want to find the information they're looking for as quickly as possible. Keep your most important content no more than two clicks away from your home page. Any deeper than this and it will be overlooked.

Include a Site Counter

This number, appearing at the bottom of a page, shows how many visitors have visited your site. Unless your site experiences massive traffic, these kinds of numbers work against you. Imagine coming across a site and seeing you are the 749th visitor. What impression would that leave you with?

Don't Include a Search Box for the Site

According to Jakob Nielsen, 50 percent of all Web site visitors are search-dominant. This means they arrive at a Web site fully expecting to use a search box to find what they are looking for at the site. What does this mean? If your site has a fair amount of content, you should provide a search box that's above the fold (viewable without any scrolling), easy to find (the upper left-hand corner is the most common placement for the search box), and comprehensive in its results.

Five Ways to Improve Your Web Site's Readability

1. *Choose background and text colors carefully.* Dark-colored text on a light-colored background (black type on a white background) is easier to read than light-colored text on a dark-colored background (white type on a black background). When in doubt, choose white as a background color and black type.
2. *Keep your type size at 11 points or larger.* Text that's too small will turn off your readers.
3. *Keep text aligned to the left.* Don't center your body text. This should only be done with headlines. The standard for most international Web sites is to have flush-left text. Stay with this.
4. *Use graphics sparingly.* According to Jakob Nielsen, author of *Homepage Usability,* 5 percent to 15 percent of a site's home page should be devoted to graphics. This creates enough visual interest but doesn't overburden the reader with download issues. Focus instead on what you say and how you say it.
5. *Keep hyperlinks blue.* According to Nielsen, 60 percent of surveyed sites use blue as the standard color for hyperlinks.

SOME QUICK TIPS TO IMPROVE YOUR
WEB SITE CONTENT

- *Use a tagline.* You have just ten seconds to capture and keep a visitor's attention. A good site uses a tagline to show visitors what your site offers and how you're different from your competitors. Put the tagline in the header section right under or beside your company name.
- *Keep text short.* Recent statistics show that people read from computer screens 25 percent slower than from paper. To address this, break up your Web site copy into small blocks, use shorter paragraphs, lead off text sections with subheads, and occasionally use bulleted lists.
- *Keep key content "above the fold."* This term is borrowed from the newspaper industry and refers to what the viewer sees on the screen on arriving at a Web site's home page. Keep key content, like your top three tasks, above the fold on your Web site's home page.
- *Provide a FAQ section.* For recurring questions, a FAQ section can be a godsend. Also, a FAQ section will help first-time visitors become acquainted with your company and its philosophy faster.
- *Provide contact information on every page.* Many people print pages from a Web site for further review. They may end up contacting you directly from that printed piece of paper, so include your company's address, telephone numbers, and e-mail at the bottom of each Web page.
- *Have a privacy policy.* If you collect any customer information (e-mail, address, telephone number), clearly state your privacy policy. People are inherently distrustful of marketers these days and stating your privacy policy will help assuage them, at least a bit.

TIPS FOR STANDOUT WEB SITE DESIGNS

- *Place your logo in the upper left.* Some 84 percent of all sites feature their logos here, so this is as close to a standard convention as you'll find on the Web.
- *Run navigational tasks down the left-hand side or across the top with tabs.* Approximately 60 percent of all sites use either of these navigation schemes.
- *Indicate download times for multimedia files.* If you're going to use Flash animation, video files, and audio files, indicate (in parentheses) how big the application is, along with an approximate time it will take to download.

- *Strategically order your tabs.* Put the information people are looking for most often on the highest-visibility tabs.
- *Don't make users scroll horizontally.* This is annoying.
- *Keep the Web page layout consistent throughout your site.* I disagree with those who say the home page template should differ from the site's interior pages. In my mind, all pages, images, elements, typefaces, headings, and footers should be consistent throughout your site. Consistency is the great multiplier to a company's identity.

LIPE'S LAW OF WEB SITES

Hire someone half your age to critique your company's site. You'll gain valuable insights into the way the younger generation uses the Web, and maybe learn about a couple of new bands.

VIEW YOUR SITE FROM DIFFERENT VANTAGE POINTS

Computers, Internet connections, monitors, and browsers vary widely. As your site is being developed, take a break and drive to the public library where you can check out the site on its computers. Then pull up a chair at your local coffee bar's computer terminal and view the site from there. The next time you visit your significant other in his or her office, log on to a computer and check out your site. From any of these vantage points, you can catch things that might otherwise go unnoticed on your own computer screen.

USE OUTSIDERS TO HELP

Does this sound familiar? Your company's president hires his brother (who just happens to be "in between jobs") to develop the company Web site. The brother spends a lot of time meeting with the staff and even more time behind his computer. The lights in the building dim every so often. Halfway through the project, no one likes the site's layout, everyone wonders why it's taking so long, and the budget now has three extra zeroes after it.

I see this situation all the time and, I've got to say, it *can* be avoided. Bring in a qualified professional to develop your Web site from the outset. When you outsource a project like this, you can capitalize on this outside person's expertise. You may end up with a site that looks a little bit different from what you had envisioned, but that's good. You (and your brother) are too close to the forest to see the trees. Hire an outsider and let her help you stand back.

CHAPTER WRAP

We are increasingly becoming an online society where a Web site is no longer an option but a necessity. If your company doesn't have a Web site, you're already falling behind. If your company's Web site is woefully inadequate, redesign it. It's forming impressions with buyers from around the world 24 hours a day.

20

THE ELEVATOR SPEECH

Your No-Cost Audio Commercial

The definition of insanity is doing the same thing over and over again and expecting a different result.

ALBERT EINSTEIN

These days, networking has become all the rage as a lead-generation tool for businesses. If you spend any time at all at networking events you'll want to pay attention to the personal introduction you use— also called your elevator speech. These ten seconds, more often than not, will end up being a make-or-break moment for your company identity. Don't make the same mistakes that 95 percent of the people do with their elevator speeches. Read on to discover how to craft an effective sound bite for your company.

WHAT IS AN ELEVATOR SPEECH?

An elevator speech is a short description of what you do that is told to someone else in the time it takes an elevator to go from the bottom floor to the top. It's the traditional way that business associates introduce themselves to one another and answers the question, "What do *you* do for a living?" Good elevator speeches last about ten seconds and should contain enough creativity and information so they're remembered long after they're given.

THE WORST THING YOU CAN DO

When asked "What do you do?" the worst answer you can give is "I'm an _____" (accountant, lawyer, consultant, or whatever). Answering like this only tells your listener what you are, not how you help others. In addition, labeling yourself just encourages the listener to lump you in with all the rest of the accountants, lawyers, or consultants. When you label yourself this way, you forgo any discussion of the benefits you provide to others and leave this up to the listener to figure on his or her own. Ninety-five percent of all people mishandle their elevator speeches, but you don't have to be one of them.

FOUR STEPS TO GIVING A WINNING ELEVATOR SPEECH

A good elevator speech is made up of three distinct parts: the hook, deliverables, benefits, and the fourth step—where you put it all together. Follow these next steps to develop an elevator speech that turns heads.

Step 1—Develop Your Own Hook

A hook is a catch phrase used to get someone's attention. Figure 20.1 provides some examples of memorable hooks.

If you were to use any of these hooks to answer the question "What do you do?" I'm confident you'd earn your listener's attention. Each one of these statements begs the next question, "How do you do that?"

Whether you open with a provocative statement, a bit of mystery, or something funny, the objective is the same—to grab a stranger's attention. Use a separate piece of paper and brainstorm on possible hooks using the format that follows:

FIGURE 20.1 *Memorable Hooks*

Occupation	Hook
Landscape gardener	I turn the world green.
Midwife	I bring life into this world.
Nutritionist	I teach people how to behave in front of food.
IRS agent	I'm a government fund-raiser.
Pilot	I shrink the globe.
Lawyer	I empower the powerless.
Politician	I'm a servant of the people.
Voice coach	I give voice to the timid.
Schoolteacher	I'm empowering the next generation.

Elevator Pitch

Step 1—Use a hook to capture attention

I'm the _____ that _____.
　　　　　[line of work you're in]　　　　　　*[hook]*

I work with _____s that _____

_____.

Step 2—Explain Your Deliverables

The next section of your elevator speech is where you explain what your service (or product) provides.

Elevator Pitch

Step 2—Explain your deliverables

I specialize in _____ for the
　　　　　　[action verb followed by your deliverables]

_____.
　　[your target market]

We sell a _____ that can _____.
　　　　[product description]　　　　　　　　*[benefits]*

Here are some examples of deliverable statements:

- I facilitate off-site strategy development sessions for nonprofits.
- I develop brochures, annual reports, and flyers for midsize companies.
- I specialize in writing ads for the banking industry.
- We sell a mower that automatically moves at the same pace you walk.

Step 3—Explain Your Benefits

The final step is to draw up a statement that covers the benefits of your product or service.

Elevator Pitch
Step 3—Explain your benefits

I help _____s
             [audience type]

_____. I _____
     [benefit]   *[action verb followed by audience type]*

_____.
     [benefit]

Here are some examples of benefit statements that will get attention:

- I help companies stop overpaying on their taxes (accountant).
- I help companies plan for growth (marketing consultant).
- I put a company's story into words (writer).
- I help business owners visually capture their identity (graphic designer).
- We help Laundromat owners make more money from their stores (laundry equipment distributors).
- We provide the capital for businesses to grow (banker).

FINAL STEP—PUTTING IT ALL TOGETHER

Now all you do is blend the three sections—your hook, deliverables, and benefit statement—into your final elevator speech.

Elevator Pitch (for a service)
Final

I'm the _____ that _____. (Step 1)
I specialize in _____ for the _____. (Step 2)
In the end, I help _____s _____. (Step 3)

Here are a couple of examples that could be used in response to the question, "What do *you* do?"

- For an accountant: *I help companies find puddles of money. I specialize in helping small companies with their tax returns. As a result of working with me, these companies free up as much cash as possible to use in growing their businesses.*
- For a nutritionist: *I teach people how to behave in front of food. I work with people who want to change their eating habits but don't know where to start. As a result, my clients lose weight, have more energy, and enjoy life more.*

CHAPTER WRAP

Draw up several elevator speeches and then try them out at the next networking event you attend. Notice how each one is received by the audience. Make changes and revisions and then commit them to memory. It may just be the most important ten seconds of your company's identity.

Part Six

FOLLOWING THROUGH

Putting the Lessons to Work

21

HOW TO SUCCESSFULLY IMPLEMENT ANY MARKETING EFFORT

Between saying and doing, many a pair of shoes is worn out.

ITALIAN PROVERB

Some business leaders I meet with wax philosophical about their marketing plans and get darn near misty-eyed as they talk about their marketing strategies. When I ask to see their implementation plan, though, they look at me like cows gazing at a passing train.

I've been on the inside of hundreds of companies, from Fortune 500 behemoths to one-person shops. I've met with executives of international organizations and marketing executives with 40+ years of experience, and the one thing they all have in common regarding their marketing is this: *they work at it.*

TIPS ON IMPLEMENTING YOUR PLAN

- *Choose your lead dog carefully. Who* is in charge of implementing your marketing effort is just as important as *what* gets implemented. To find the right

The Top Ten Signs Your Marketing Implementation Needs Help

10. When callers ask who handles your marketing, the receptionist answers, "I'm not really sure."
9. Not one of your company's marketers has project management experience.
8. Silence greets the question, "How many new leads have we generated this month?"
7. The typestyles and colors for your company's brochure, Web site, and business cards vary widely.
6. The official deadline for finishing your new Web site is "Whenever it gets done."
5. All your company identity work has been developed in-house.
4. You can't answer the question, "How much does your company spend to get a new lead?"
3. Your CFO is your company's chief marketer.
2. His secretary runs the marketing committee meetings.
1. No one attends these meetings.

marketing leader, first identify all the possible candidates in your company who think strategically and act decisively. In smaller businesses, there may only be one candidate: the owner. In larger companies, you'll have a wider field to choose from.

- *The recipe for a successful marketer.* When I'm asked to describe the personality of a successful marketer, here's how I respond: start with a dose of project manager, stir in some accountant, mix in a dash of salesperson, blend in a pinch of chemistry professor, sprinkle with a touch of high-wire acrobat, add a twist of ice-in-your-veins commodities broker, then top it all off with some lounge entertainer. Simmer for approximately 20 years; the flavor gets better with age.

THE TOP THREE QUALITIES YOU'LL FIND IN EVERY IMPLEMENTER

1. Initiative

Your chief marketing implementer will face a host of challenges (e.g., "We ran out of the paper stock you wanted," "The vendor who was printing our brochure has filed for bankruptcy," "Our database was accidentally deleted"), so it's important that this person be able to think creatively under fire.

2. Organizational Skills

As a child, I watched *The Ed Sullivan Show* on television. Some of these episodes would feature a plate spinner as a guest. Remember him? He'd start a plate spinning and place it on the top of a three-foot dowel rod. After the first plate was spinning smoothly, he'd spin another plate and set it on another dowel rod. After about a minute, the spinner would have 10 to 15 plates spinning simultaneously.

It really became interesting when one of the plates started losing its momentum and began to wobble. Everybody in the audience held their breath, expecting the plate to come crashing down. Just in the nick of time, the plate spinner, with a flick of his wrist, would spin the plate back to life. As soon as this happened, another plate would start to wobble. And so on it went.

Your marketing leader is your company's plate spinner. Each of the plates will be a separate marketing project and every so often, she'll have to spin a project back to life to keep the overall effort on track.

3. Get-Along Skills

Marketers work with the widest array of people: from vendors to customers, accountants to sales representatives, administrative staff to executives, a marketer interacts with every conceivable type of personality, often within the same hour. Your company's marketer must have an inner self-confidence and good get-along skills.

THE NUMBER ONE MISTAKE WHEN HIRING MARKETERS

When I meet the marketing staff at a new client, I always ask about their background. Invariably, I learn that the person responsible for implementing marketing projects was initially hired for her graphic design background. After being brought in to work on designing new ads, she was assigned the task of designing a new marketing brochure.

About this time, the sales manager started complaining to her about the lack of a distributor on the East Coast. The following week, the finance director wondered aloud why product margins were falling. A week after that, the IT department approached her about launching an e-commerce Web site. Meanwhile, the R&D engineers approached her, after learning that a key competitor was stealing market share, and wondered aloud why they hadn't launched their own new product. Everyone seemed to ask, all at the same time, "What is marketing going to do?" Poor designer!

What started as the ideal marketing *design* job for her (designing ads, creating brochures) had morphed overnight into a *real* marketing job—complete with issues of pricing, product development, distribution, and strategic promotional mix.

Even if you have a raft of new ads or brochures that rest in your to-do pile, resist the temptation—with every bone in your body—to hire a graphic designer. Instead, hire someone with a marketing background and a proven ability to manage projects. Graphic designers like to *design* things, not manage projects.

PROJECT MANAGEMENT IS THE GROUNDING

Talk to a professional writer and chances are she cut her teeth writing short stories. Talk to a professional football player and you'll learn he's spent countless hours working on his blocking and tackling. Every art has its grounding and marketing's grounding is *project management*. Because so much of marketing is managing projects, the really good marketers boast years of project management experience. When you start looking at résumés for that inevitable marketing opening, ask yourself these questions:

- What projects has this person managed from start to finish?
- Did she manage numerous projects concurrently?
- Was this person the project leader for these projects or just a team member?

CHANGE IS A NECESSARY INGREDIENT

In a widely quoted article in *Fast Company* magazine, Dr. Edward Miller, dean of the medical school and CEO of the hospital at Johns Hopkins University, presented some startling statistics. He showed that close to 600,000 people have coronary bypass operations each year in the United States. Half of the time, the grafts become clogged again, requiring additional surgery. Many bypass patients can avoid this second surgery if they just adopted a healthier lifestyle, but they don't.

Dr. Miller explained, "If you look at people after coronary-artery bypass grafting two years later, 90 percent of them [the patients] have not changed their lifestyles . . . Even though they know they have a very bad disease, and they know they should change their lifestyle, they can't." Remember this the next time you launch a brand-new marketing initiative. You're sure to encounter this human aversion to change, and you'll often find that those people you most need for sign-offs and approvals are the very ones who put up the most roadblocks. You *will* be tested by those who oppose change, but the true mark of a successful marketer is how well you can rise above them.

WAYS TO ATTACK PROCRASTINATION

I recently worked with a brick-and-mortar retail company to help it establish an e-commerce Web site. At the point where the owners had to write copy for more than 150 products, they froze. The project just seemed so overwhelming. So I suggested they start by writing copy for one category of products and their demeanor brightened immediately. After they finished writing the copy for that first category, we loaded those products and turned them on for sale. This way, the owners could see a tangible result (sales) from accomplishing a subtask. If you're stuck trying to complete a certain task, try breaking it down into more manageable subtasks, with a reward waiting for you after completing the subtask.

Block Off the Same Time, Same Day

Many successful marketers invariably block off the same day and time to work on their marketing tasks. For me, I've found that Friday afternoons work best because my telephone stops ringing and I'm seldom invited to Friday afternoon meetings.

FOUR THINGS YOU *MUST* DO TO SUCCESSFULLY IMPLEMENT YOUR MARKETING PROJECTS

1. Use a Day-Planning System

To help you manage the myriad details of your projects, use some type of day-planning system. Whether it's paper-based or electronic is up to you, but without some basic project management tool like this, your implementation efforts will be doomed from the start. I found this out when I was a marketing assistant on a product with a $60 million marketing budget. Pretty soon, my to-do list covered three full pages, single-spaced. In short, my planning tools weren't sophisticated enough to tackle the tasks at hand.

Luckily, I enrolled in a Franklin Covey seminar that taught me the basics of time management and gave me the most valuable planning tool I've found—a Franklin Day Planner. If you're interested in learning more about this great marketing tool, visit *www.franklincovey.com.*

Don't wait until you're snowed under to make the same mistake. Employ a day-planning system and take the time to understand how it will work best for you. With this as a tool in your implementation tool kit, you'll find your marketing abilities will improve exponentially.

2. Plan for Contingencies

When a pilot draws up a flight plan, he identifies alternate airports along the route. Then, if he is faced with an emergency, he can divert to the alternate airport and land safely. Is this being pessimistic? No, it's being realistic. Some believe it's pessimistic to ask, "What could go wrong?" Not me. When you ask that question, you put people through the process of visualizing possible mistakes—and fixes.

3. Hold Regular Project Meetings

When I was a marketing director during my corporate career, I insisted on bi-weekly project meetings with my staff. During these meetings, the staff would update each other (and me) on each project's status. These meetings are important for communication's sake.

But the *preparation* that occurs before these meetings is the real payoff. No one wants to look stupid in front of his or her peers, or boss. So they check, recheck and triple-check deadlines and commitments before the meeting.

4. Honor Deadlines

I'm a stickler on this for several reasons. First, when you develop a marketing plan, your deadlines reflect strategic details of your business (e.g., seasonality, supply logistics). So when you miss a deadline, you actually water down the strategy behind that deadline.

Missing deadlines also damages your credibility. Credibility with your boss, your board, your investors, and even your fellow workers will suffer if you constantly miss deadlines.

Finally, missing deadlines allows complacency to creep into your operations. Miss enough deadlines, and *no one* takes them seriously.

THE FIVE MOST POWERFUL WORDS FOR SUCCESSFUL IMPLEMENTATION

I once worked with the savvy president of a travel incentive company and she always closed a meeting by asking, *"What are our next steps?"* From her I learned that these are the five most powerful words for successful implementation.

At the end of every marketing meeting, ask *"What are our next steps?"* When you ask this question, you (1) create the expectation that follow-through is needed, (2) identify exactly which steps are to follow, and (3) clarify who is responsible for accomplishing them.

HOW TO BETTER MANAGE DEADLINES

First, establish your *drop-dead date*. This is the last date you, or anyone in your company, can "touch" a marketing vehicle (e.g., the proof on a direct-mail piece) before you hand it over to an outside vendor. Memorize this drop-dead date, and then don't tell anyone what it is.

Next, establish another date that is five business days before the drop-dead date. This is your *published deadline* and should be communicated to everyone whose input you'll need. This date (with its fudge factor) gives you a cushion in case things get offtrack or you run into an unplanned incident (e.g., the president is called away suddenly on business or the printer runs out of your paper stock).

COPY YOURSELF ON ALL MARKETING CAMPAIGNS

For one client, I developed an outer envelope of a direct-mail piece with some teaser copy on it. It looked fine to the client and to me as it went to press. When I received my copy of the direct-mail package at home, I saw (much to my chagrin) that the post office had applied a bar code sticker *right over* the teaser copy. You couldn't even read it. Sure, this was disappointing, but because my name was on the mailing list, I learned a valuable lesson that day—all teaser copy must appear at least ⅝ths of an inch above the bottom of a direct-mail piece.

By adding your name to your company's mailing list (or promotional e-mail list), you'll view your marketing effort *exactly* the same way your buyers do.

ELIMINATE ONE MARKETING TASK EACH YEAR

I can't count the number of stressed-out marketers I've seen over the past 20 years. As task after task is added to their plates (the test launch in Albuquerque, new packaging for the Gizmo line, a new set of budget reports), nothing is ever removed.

Stop this madness at once, and identify one task to eliminate every year. All too often, a task gets hard-coded into a company's operation (e.g., issuing a department report), yet it provides no redeeming value to the organization. What everyone's forgotten is that somebody (the marketer) sinks boatloads of time into these tasks, without any benefit. So look hard for one marketing task you can eliminate in the year ahead. Your health and sanity depend on it.

ALWAYS HAVE HARD-COPY BACKUP

When I was a graduate student in the 1980s, we had "Interview Season" each spring. During this hectic two-month period, Fortune 500 companies would traipse through the Northwestern University campus looking for fresh recruits.

The companies would put on dog-and-pony shows at a local hotel during the evening. At these presentations, senior managers from a company would regale us with tales of how exciting it is to work for this particular company. The presentations typically took the form of speeches with question-and-answer periods afterwards. This one night, though, was totally different.

That night, I shuffled in, along with about 150 other eager students, to listen to the presentation of a major consumer foods company based on the East Coast. What first caught my eye was the amazing array of electronic equipment set up in the middle of the room. Two side-by-side slide projectors, a jumble of huge speakers, and a mass of wires told me that this presentation would be different from the others.

After an overzealous senior executive welcomed us, he promised that we were in for the presentation of a lifetime. As the lights dimmed, I excitedly leaned forward in my chair and felt butterflies batting around in my stomach. What happened next was the real knockout punch.

I heard a few clicks and whirrs, and then a loud explosion accompanied by a brilliant flash of light. Suddenly, the room was shrouded in darkness.

So, there we were, me and 150 of the smartest people I knew, sitting in a room with Fortune 500 executives scurrying about trying to salvage their equipment . . . and reputations. Shortly after, the presentation was canceled.

Looking back on that incident, I realize there's a valuable lesson for all businesses: always have hard-copy backup for any presentation. Maybe that night if we'd been herded into another room and given handouts of the presentation, the show could have gone on. But it didn't, and I still think about that company in terms of that disastrous presentation.

MAKE SURE YOUR MARKETING IS INTEGRATED

I once helped develop a marketing campaign for a high-end town home development. We created very professional print ads and placed them in more than ten publications. We aired radio spots on a popular morning show. We bought space on inside digital media screens. We developed a professional Web site and organized several special events to generate qualified leads. In short, we poured tons of time and money into motivating people to visit this new property.

Unfortunately, all this went to waste because the real estate developer dragged his feet in setting up a high-quality demonstration unit (a sample town home). As a result, all the people who responded to our ads, commercials, and special events were shown a unit that was unfurnished and underwhelming.

This is one example of how a marketing effort can stumble without integrated execution. For this property's identity to stand out from the crowd, a high-quality demonstration unit should have been in place from day one.

Carry the battle to them. Don't let them bring it to you.

HARRY TRUMAN, 33rd U.S. President

Can You Hear Your Momentum?

Several years ago, I was brought in to help improve the marketing activities for a large leisure-travel agency. When I arrived, the agency had a phone system that filled the air with ringing sounds on a busy day. Because our ads were placed in Sunday travel sections of newspapers, all day Monday was filled with the sounds of ringing phones.

Then one day, the company switched vendors and a new phone system was installed. The signal for an incoming call was no longer a ring tone; it was instead a silent flashing light. No ring sound whatsoever. That following Monday I walked into the offices and was greeted with deathly silence. The phones were as busy as ever, but you could have heard a pin drop. Agents were talking in hushed whispers and the lack of sound put a real damper on their mood. Personally, it drove me crazy because I had no way of gauging the business's activity level. Sadly, the agency closed a few years later.

SOME TIPS ON HOW TO GET THE VERY BEST OUT OF A DESIGN FIRM

Understand The Design Firm's Philosophy

When interviewing design firms, ask them to explain their design philosophy. Some will answer thoughtfully. Others will flap around like a trout on a sidewalk. If a creative firm can't clearly articulate its design philosophy, then working with the firm may be just as confusing.

Develop a Creative Brief

If you work with an outside firm to design your company identity, you'll be asking it to capture your company's personality. To help the firm with this important task, draw up a one-page creative brief that captures these elements of your company identity:

- Target audience
- Company positioning
- Key messages

The firm will be able to funnel this thinking into its deliverables and you'll end up with results that are more in tune with your objectives.

Point Out the Sacred Cows

Any company identity project comes with a history. If certain identity elements (e.g., name, logo, tagline, colors, typestyles)—also called *sacred cows—can't* be touched by the design firm, point these out *before* the project begins.

Be Honest and Upfront about the Project Budget

Tell the firm, honestly, exactly what you can afford to spend on this project. This helps guide an outside firm's thinking towards your project. For example, if a Web site design firm knows that its budget is less than $5,000, it can reasonably eliminate features such as Flash animation work from consideration.

Show Examples of Work You Like

Outside firms hate to read minds. If you can show the firm some examples of work you like, you will help point the firm in a certain direction—your direction.

CHAPTER WRAP

I recently saw a Dilbert cartoon with the caption, *"I love deadlines. I especially like the whooshing sound they make as they go flying by."* At first blush, this is funny. After

LIPE'S LAW OF IMPLEMENTATION

Every task in your marketing plan must have a corresponding:

1. Project leader
2. Start date
3. End date
4. Expected cost

These will help you know *how* every item will get accomplished, rather than just *what* is going to get accomplished.

two decades in the marketing business, I can also tell you it's true. Most marketing efforts don't fail from a lack of thought; they fail from a lack of execution.

Don't leave your best-laid plans to chance. Develop a process for implementation and then assign the very best project manager at your company to get the job done.

The greatest plan in the world won't mean diddly-squat unless time and attention are devoted to implementing it. Successful marketing efforts don't result from kismet or fate; someone works hard at implementing them—day in and day out.

22

METRICS

The Numbers You Must Know to Measure Your Effort

In the long run, men hit only what they aim at.

HENRY DAVID THOREAU

When I worked in sales for a computer software company, we would place ads in national business publications to generate leads. Each ad featured, at the very bottom, our toll-free 800 number and the phrase "Please ask for Sandy Hills." The funny thing was that there was no such person named Sandy Hills. It was a fictitious name designed to tip off our receptionist that the caller was a lead responding to the print ad. Every month, our receptionist would count the number of Sandy Hills requests and report back this number to us. Little did I know that this was my first exposure to marketing metrics and the role it can play in analyzing a marketing effort.

WHAT METRICS DO FOR A COMPANY

Once your company starts using metrics for any period of time, you'll begin to think in a more disciplined way about your marketing. You'll find yourself (or your staff) asking more detailed questions about your marketing efforts—questions that follow a logical train of thought. Not surprisingly, the answers that spring from this process will spur you on to an even greater strategic understanding of your marketing.

For example, let's say you're analyzing your company's marketing efforts and you notice that you've generated a substantial number of leads but are having trouble converting them into sales. This information, which originates from an analysis of your monthly metrics, may lead you to the following questions:

- Do we have an issue with our prices?
- Do we lack a device like a money-back guarantee to help close sales?
- Do our sales materials do an effective job of persuading readers to purchase from us?
- Do our salespeople need more training on closing techniques?
- Do our products come up short against our competitors?

Once you dig deeper into this set of strategic questions, you'll likely identify a marketing problem that must be fixed. Then you can step back and celebrate that your marketing effort has shifted from reactive to proactive. Your marketing is now anchored in action rather than reaction.

Marketing metrics that can help you arrive at this stage fall into two broad classes:

1. Marketing health metrics
2. Performance metrics

Let's take them one at a time.

SOME BASIC MARKETING HEALTH METRICS

Marketing health metrics are designed to help you take the pulse of your company's marketing and are particularly good at identifying areas for further analysis. Some of the more common marketing health metrics are:

- New inquiries
- Source of leads

- New customer sales
- New product revenue
- Profitability by project

New Inquiries

Inquiries (or leads) are the lifeblood, the energy source, of a company's marketing endeavors. Because some new leads ultimately turn into new customers, you'll learn to crave new leads like a fire craves oxygen. The most common inquiries are:

- Calling and requesting a brochure
- Leaving a business card at your trade show booth
- E-mailing you with a question
- Sending in a reply card
- Registering on your Web site
- Getting your name from someone else
- Signing up for an e-newsletter

You'll want to measure and report on the monthly numbers of inquiries for your company. Over time, you'll start noticing patterns for these numbers and this knowledge will help you shed light on such additional questions as:

- What is the seasonality of our business?
- Which months generate the most leads for us? Why?
- Which programs generate the most leads for us? Why?

Tracking your company's leads less than monthly is dangerous because you may not give yourself adequate time to react to market changes. For example, if your business enjoys a strong winter seasonality (e.g., a snowplowing service, hot cereals), and you calculate metrics quarterly, then more than half your selling season will be over before you can react to any learning. This leaves you precious little time to take corrective actions, if needed.

Source of Leads

Just as important as how many leads you get is *where they come from*. Every month, analyze your leads by their source. A lead source report might look something like this:

February Lead Sources

Source	# of leads	% of leads
Referrals	10	40%
Direct mail	7	28%
Yellow pages	5	20%
Web site	3	12%
Total	25	100%

Over the course of a few months, you'll start to single out those programs that produce the most leads and those that don't. From this knowledge, you can then redirect funds (and time) from underperforming programs to ones that are performing well.

New Customer Sales

Every business experiences customer attrition. Some customers may start buying from your competitors. Some customers move away. Some die. Plan on this kind of customer turnover; it's a fact of life in the business world. To counteract this phenomenon, your marketing must have a built-in mechanism designed to provide a continual stream of new customers to replace those you've lost.

First, define a new customer as one who has conducted business with you for 24 months or less. Then generate a quick report showing your new customers, ranked by sales—high to low—and where they came from. The report might look like this:

New Customer Report—Annual

Customer	Annual Sales	Source
XYZ Inc.	$ 300,000	Yellow Pages
ABC Co.	$ 240,000	Referral–trade assn.
Climb On Inc.	$ 174,000	Yellow Pages
On Belay Inc.	$ 124,000	Referral–ABC Co.
Beasley's	$ 94,000	Direct mail

Prepare this report every January for the preceding year and you'll start to see where your new customers come from and what attracts them to your door. Using the previous example, what preliminary conclusions could you draw?

New Product Revenue

When I worked for a large consumer goods company, we religiously tracked new product revenue (revenue from products launched within the past five years). This was an important barometer because new products and services intrigue buyers. You could generate a report at the end of every year that breaks down your company's sales by new and old product revenue.

Profitability by Project

It's good to know your sales picture. It's even better to know your profit picture. If your business is project-oriented (e.g., a consulting practice or an engineering firm), calculate your firm's profitability by project for a year's worth of projects.

To do this, take all the revenue for a project and then subtract all the direct costs associated with the project. The remaining amount is your *total project profit*. Now, as a second step, divide the total project profit by the total project revenue number and you'll arrive at a *profit margin* percentage.

For example:

	Profit Margin Calculation
Total project revenue	$7,500
Less total project costs	$2,190
Equals gross profit	$5,310 (gross profit)
Divided by total project revenue	$5,310/$7,500
Equals gross profit margin	71% (gross margin)

After calculating this gross profit margin for a variety of projects, you'll start to notice that some projects are more profitable than others. Why is this? Is it because of the lower costs for these project types? Can you charge higher prices for these projects?

If you're a larger company, a good cost accounting system makes this job easier. Even if you're a smaller company, you can still arrive at these metrics with a little digging and a good calculator. Once you do this exercise for the first time, the results will be eye-opening and you'll make it a standard practice to analyze profitability by project.

SOME OTHER HEALTH METRICS

Other metrics you might use in this marketing health category are:

- Sales calls per week
- Presentations per week
- Proposals per month
- Average revenues per sales call
- Number of lost customers
- Percentage of sales sold off a promotion
- Average price per sale
- Sales per employee
- Market share (that is, what percent share of the overall market your business owns)
- Close ratio (the percent of inquiries you turn into orders)

PERFORMANCE METRICS FOR YOUR MARKETING PROGRAMS

The other important set of metrics used to evaluate your marketing effort is called *performance metrics*. These measures will help identify the spending efficiencies behind your marketing—that is to say, how well your marketing money is being spent. Using some of these metrics, you'll learn which marketing programs outperform others, which are laggards, and, ultimately, which ones overall produce the biggest bang for your marketing buck. Among these measures are:

- Cost per inquiry (CPI)
- Cost per order (CPO)

Cost per Inquiry (CPI)

Also called *cost per lead,* this is a simple metric that helps determine the worth of your lead-generation programs. When I worked for a direct-marketing firm, we calculated CPIs for every single publication we advertised in, thus providing a gold mine of information about our entire print advertising campaign. From this analysis, I could tell you which publications pulled in the most inquiries, which inquiries converted to orders at the highest levels, and, finally, how much we were spending to generate a lead in our overall marketing program.

For measuring the pure efficiency and impact of your marketing spending, this metric can't be beat. Here's how you calculate it:

Cost per Inquiry Calculation

Total marketing expenses for a program	$2,500
Divided by total inquiries	15
Equals cost per inquiry (CPI)	$166

The total marketing expenses for a program can include any of the following:

- Graphic design costs
- Copywriting costs
- Printing
- Postage
- Trade show costs
- Web site development and maintenance costs
- Media placement (e.g., offline and online ads)
- Pay-for-performance costs (e.g., pay-per-click)
- Consultant costs
- Publicity costs

Now, if the past year's cost-per-inquiry number was $250 (versus this year's $166), your marketing is improving because the costs of acquiring a lead are falling. Conversely, if this year's figure is higher than the past year's, your marketing is less efficient and you'll need to determine why this is.

For companies with multiple product lines, or a wide variety of marketing programs, you may want to take this analysis one step further by calculating CPIs for each product line or marketing program.

Cost per Order (CPO)

At the same time you're calculating your CPI, you can also calculate your *cost per order*. Calculate your CPO like this:

Cost per Order Calculation

Total marketing expenses for a program	$2,500
Divided by total orders	5
Equals cost per order (CPO)	$500

While CPI is a measure of how well you're spending to get inquiries, CPO measures how efficient you are in obtaining *orders*. CPO, as a number, is always higher than CPI because a business receives more inquiries than orders. If your CPO is significantly higher than your CPI (for example, ten times higher or more), this may mean your company has trouble converting inquiries into orders (e.g., poor closing techniques by your sales force, substandard product features versus the competition, your company lacks certain marketing tools).

HOW TO CALCULATE A PROGRAM'S BREAKEVEN

As you become more comfortable with your company's metrics, eventually you'll want to calculate *break-even levels* for each marketing program. The break-even point is a number you calculate *before* a program runs that identifies the number of orders necessary to cover all the costs for the program. Here's how you calculate it:

	How to Calculate a Breakeven
Total marketing expenses for a program	$2,950
Average profit from a sale	$500
Divide marketing expenses by average profit	$2,950/$500
Equals break-even orders	5.9 or 6 orders

OTHER BENEFITS OF PROGRAMS, PAST BREAKEVEN

Remember that marketing programs often have more than one objective. Companies tend to focus rigidly on breakeven, to the exclusion of other important benefits. For example, if you're planning for a trade show, not only could you develop a breakeven for the program, but you might also establish other quantifiable objectives such as:

- New contacts made
- Number of business cards collected
- Number of demonstrations given

Often a marketing program needs time (sometimes years) to generate a breakeven, yet during those early years, the program is generating valuable marketing benefits for the company. For every marketing program, I recommend having at least one other quantifiable benefit, besides breakeven, that you want to achieve.

The Top Ten Web Site Performance Indicators

According to Jupiter Research, more than 70 percent of companies don't deliver important Web data to senior executives, and more than 80 percent don't report data to merchandising staff. Using key performance indicators (KPIs) to measure the impact of your Web site will force you to constantly improve its performance. Here are ten of the most important metrics every Web site should be tracking:

10. Busiest periods (in hour intervals) of day for your site
9. Page views per day
8. Average page views per visitor
7. Most popular pages on the site
6. Common search phrases used to arrive at the site
5. Most common site entry page
4. Most common site exit page
3. Most requested pages
2. Top referring sites
1. Unique visitors per day

REALIZE THE INTANGIBLES

Here's a pop quiz:

- How can you measure your company's awareness?
- How do you measure the credibility you've created with buyers?
- How would you track word-of-mouth mentions from a marketing campaign?

The answer to all three is . . . you *can't*. These are examples of qualitative benefits and they reinforce the notion that marketing isn't always black and white. Resign yourself to this fact: some aspects of your company's marketing can't *ever* be measured, but they also can't be ignored. Your Chief Financial Officer won't like this answer, but it's true.

ONE QUESTION YOU MUST ASK EVERY NEW PROSPECT

Any time a new buyer approaches your company, the first question you should ask is: *How did you hear about us?*

The answer to this question becomes a window into the workings of your marketing machine. If enough of these buyers answer that they saw your ad in *XYZ* magazine, then you know that marketing vehicle is a winner.

One of the best answers you'll ever hear to this question is "Geez, I don't know. I see you everywhere. There was the ad in *XYZ* magazine. Then I saw your booth at the ABC trade show. And then someone forwarded me an e-mail from your company." An answer like this means your company has a truly integrated marketing campaign, hitting on all cylinders.

LIPE'S LAW OF METRICS

When a buyer tells you he or she learned about your company from multiple sources (e.g., "Well, my friend told me about you initially, I receive your catalogs, *and* I just saw your billboard on my way home from work."), which is the most accurate source for that lead? Referral? Direct mail? Or billboards? If your lead source tracking system allows, *check all three*. Each played a part in generating the order. If you can't check three, check the first one mentioned.

THREE OUTSTANDING WAYS TO CAPTURE METRICS

1. *Add a "Lead Source" box to your sales order paperwork.* When a salesperson has to process paperwork for a specific order, make him check a box identifying how the prospect came to him. If you want to really add teeth to this method, enforce a rule that no order paperwork will be processed without a lead source being identified.

2. *Distribute preprinted telephone notepads to your sales force.* Using a handy device like this, a salesperson can check off the source of the lead, while she carries on a conversation with the prospect.

3. *Add key codes to your promotional pieces.* We've all been asked by a catalog company to read over the telephone the "key code found on the back cover." There's a reason. Once that code is put into the computer, it identifies which marketing catalog the buyer has, so that the marketing department can determine which are the most effective catalogs. Try adding a unique code to any promotional piece, then train your sales staff, who will field any inquiries, to ask every respondent for the code on his or her mailer.

SCORECARDS: THE NEED FOR MONITORING

To help you collect and report on your metrics, I recommend using a marketing scorecard. The scorecard example in Figure 22.1 is one I helped develop for a client. Obviously, your metrics may be different from the ones shown here, but this is a handy format to use when reporting your data.

There are several benefits to using a marketing scorecard. First, because you can record all your marketing metrics within this standard format, tracking historical changes is easier. Second, more strategic discussion is possible when all your numbers appear in one report, side by side. Finally, presenting the metrics using a marketing scorecard further reinforces the importance of tracking metrics in your marketing.

CHAPTER WRAP

Several years ago, I visited a friend who was recuperating in the hospital. A steady stream of nurses drifted in to take her temperature, read her charts, monitor her blood pressure, and check her medicine schedules. After taking all the readings, the nurse diligently entered these measurements into a computer monitor.

Soon after, a doctor shuffled in and gazed intently at the computer, familiarizing himself with the patient's progress over the past 24 hours. As I watched this process one day, it dawned on me that this is the same process that marketers use to evaluate their marketing programs. They monitor, record, and analyze vital data, then revise their strategies or tactics based on the data they see.

If you're serious about your marketing effort, borrow a chapter from the health professionals and incorporate metrics into your effort. Your marketing effort, and company identity, will only improve.

FIGURE 22.1 *Marketing Scorecard*

Chammer Lammer, Inc.
Scorecard

Period: January '07

1. Revenue & Orders	Monthly			YTD		
	07	06	% +/–	07	06	% +/–
Revenue						
Orders						

Rationale:

> This is where your narrative would go.
> You would plug in any discussion of the numbers here.

2. Marketing	Monthly			YTD		
	07	06	% +/–	07	06	% +/–
Marketing Expenses						
Cost per Order (CPO)						

Rationale:

3. Sales	Monthly			YTD		
	07	06	% +/–	07	06	% +/–
Outbound Calls						
Inbound Calls						

Rationale:

23

SOME FINAL WORDS

I won't lie to you. Developing a standout company identity is hard work, but the payoff is enormous. Your company will benefit from greater trust, higher credibility, greater customer satisfaction, higher repeat sales, more word of mouth, and other benefits you haven't yet considered.

Although I've covered a great deal of ground in this book, I want to leave you with these four distinct lessons to start applying today.

1. GREAT IDENTITIES SPRING FROM CAREFULLY PLANNED STRATEGIES

Your company will succeed at crafting a winning brand only after it has spent time pinpointing *exactly* what kind of brand it wants. Strong marketing companies envision the end result before ever spending time on the execution. So, create an identity marketing plan for every product (or service) in your company. Budget at least 90 days for this strategic process and, in the end, wind up with a written plan that details its:

- Target audiences
- Brand identity elements
- Key messaging
- Implementation strategy

2. EVERY BRAND ELEMENT MUST BE FINELY CRAFTED

The whole is the sum of its parts. Just as a bouquet would be spoiled by a dead rose, one subpar identity element, among an array of otherwise impressive ones, could raise a red flag for a buyer.

If you want your company identity to be perceived in the best possible light, start by examining every single facet of your company identity with a critical eye. Don't ask if it's good enough. Ask instead if it's *great*.

Until you can honestly say that every piece, every element, that bears your company identity is of the highest quality, your work's not done. *Hint:* Your work is never done.

3. CONSISTENCY IS THE HALLMARK OF A SOLID IDENTITY

The more consistent your tools are, the stronger they will register. Using the same logo, tagline, typestyles, colors, design templates, key messages, copy points, and spoken words across all your branding elements is critically important. Higher consistency begets higher awareness. Your goal should be to spread all your company's identity tools out on a desk and see the exact same visuals and messages in every piece.

4. MAKE MOMENTUM YOUR FRIEND

After two decades in the marketing field, I'm constantly reminded of just how important momentum is to a successful marketing effort. Once you have it, never let it slip away. If you don't have it yet, do everything in your power to get it. If your company is small, set a goal of tackling one new marketing initiative each week, and follow the steps I recommend in Chapter 21. If your company is larger (more than $1 million in annual revenues), consider hiring a part-time or full-time resource to head up your marketing initiatives; then insist that he, too, read Chapter 21.

Once your company sets about improving its company identity and begins to acquire the slightest bit of momentum, a host of unrelated, yet significant things will spring from that process. Your company may be asked unexpectedly by a media member to provide information for a feature. You may receive a call from a buyer who, up to this point, was sitting on the fence, but now wants to place an order. Your company may suddenly start getting referrals from the graphic design agency you hired to help with your corporate identity. I can't predict what these events will be, but I can confidently predict they *will* happen. And when they do, you'll know you have momentum, and a standout company identity to back it up.

advertising Any paid form of nonpersonal communication or presentation of a product, service, idea, or company.

affinity An association or relationship (e.g., church membership) that indicates a similarity in lifestyle among individuals.

attributes The features of a product that are thought to appeal to customers.

audience Homes or individuals watching, reading, seeing, or listening to a given media vehicle.

awareness Movement of information about your product, service, or company into a prospect's conscious mind. Often the desired objective of an advertising campaign and a principal goal of public relations.

benefit The satisfaction or fulfillment of needs that a customer receives from your products or services. In "My factories make cosmetics; we sell hope," hope is the benefit.

billboard Popular name for outdoor advertising signage.

body copy The words in a marketing piece that support and amplify the headline and subhead. The purpose of the body copy is to convince someone to buy your product.

brand The combination of symbols, words, or designs that differentiate one company's product from another's. Brand is also used to describe a company's family of products. A brand of coffee, for instance, might include its regular variety as well as its decaffeinated and instant varieties.

brand awareness The extent to which a brand or brand name is recognized by potential buyers.

brand image A group of associations that a consumer attributes to a specific brand.

brand name A protected, proprietary trademark of a manufacturer or products or services.

break-even analysis The analysis of a product or service to determine the sales level required to cover both fixed costs of providing the product and the marketing and sales costs involved.

brochure A produced communication piece that's typically printed on heavier paper stock and features details about a company and its products or services.

budget The detailed financial component of a plan that guides the allocation of resources. It should also provide a means to measure deviation of actual versus desired results for analysis.

call to action A highly motivating statement that tells the reader what action he or she should take next and exactly how to do it (for example, "Call 1-800-555-1213 now to order.").

capabilities brochure Promotional brochure stating what your company does and the general capabilities you offer customers. It can include general information as well as specific details about the company and its operations.

channel A group of retailers or distributors through whom a product is distributed.

channel marketing A way of organizing marketing functions in a company that puts individuals in charge of selling to specific classes of trade.

collateral Any and all printed materials designed to support a brand or company's promotional effort.

consumer The person who actually uses the product or service. Also called a *customer, patron, buyer, shopper,* or *end user.*

contingency plan An acceptable alternative plan that can be implemented in the event a basic plan is aborted or changed for any reason.

copywriting Writing text for an ad or promotional piece.

CPI Cost per inquiry. Arrived at by dividing the total marketing costs by the number of inquiries (for example, $2,500 marketing costs/25 inquiries = $100 CPI).

CPO Cost per order. Arrived at by dividing the total marketing costs by the number of orders (for example, $2,500 marketing costs/5 orders = $500 CPO).

creative General description of the activity related to the development of promotional materials. Includes concepts, design, and copy.

customer Loosely, any buyer of a product or service, at any trade level. Also called a consumer or buyer.

customer feedback Compliments, criticisms, or general information provided to a company by its customers about products, services, or other aspects of the business.

deadline A concrete time limit. Can be used for projects, subprojects, offers (expiration date), and a variety of other marketing uses.

demographics Statistics about the socioeconomic makeup of a population, including age, gender, race, occupation, income, education.

differentiation Establishing a distinction in the mind of a customer about products, services, or a company.

direct mail Marketing materials sent directly to a prospect or customer via the U.S. Postal Service or a private delivery company.

discount A reduction in the stated rate or list price, usually offered in the form of a percentage and used as an incentive to make a purchase.

distribution The delivery or conveyance of a good or service to a market.

distribution channel The chain or intermediaries linking the producer of a good to the consumer.

domain name The text-based URL or address of a Web site. Domain names usually consist of several different segments. The name *www.emergemarketing.com,* for example, includes the generic "www" and ".com" identifiers, along with the unique name "emergemarketing."

FAQs (frequently asked questions) A list of questions and answers related to a particular software application, Web site, or issue, FAQs can help users get answers without overburdening human support staff and they can be used strategically to attract traffic in a Web site.

feature A characteristic or property of a product or service such as reliability, price, convenience, safety, quality, size.

flyer An inexpensive, one-page promotional sheet (usually 8½" × 11") typically intended for handing out or bulk mailing.

frequency How many times a person buys from you, how many times a marketing message is exposed to a target audience, or how many times a program is run.

front end All marketing activities designed to generate inquiries.

gatekeeper Someone within an organization who doesn't directly consume a product or service but still wields considerable influence in the purchase decision-making process.

headline A sentence, phrase, or words that appear above a body of text. The purpose of a headline is to attract attention and prod the reader to continue reading.

home page The main (or first) page of a Web site.

hyperlink (or link) A link a user clicks on to view another Web page. Hyperlinks can appear as graphics or as areas of differently colored or underlined text.

image The way a company or organization is perceived by the public and its customers.

impressions The total number of exposures given for a particular medium.

inquiry See *lead.*

integrated marketing communications Coordination across a variety of promotional vehicles that ensures all marketing messages are clear and consistent. The outcome of integrated communications is *synergy*.

Internet A network of networks, built on a set of widely used software protocols that link millions of computers around the world. Services such as e-mail and the Web use the Internet to transfer data.

JPEG (Joint Photographic Experts Group) One of the two most common image types used on the Web. (GIF is the other.) JPEG is used mostly for photographic reproductions. Also referred to as jpg.

keywords Descriptive words that are embedded in a Web site code and throughout Web site copy.

lead A new and unqualified prospect or client, previously unknown to a salesperson or company. Also called an *inquiry*.

lead generation Marketing tactics used to solicit leads for sales follow-up; includes direct mailings, trade shows, networking, and others.

leave-behind Documents or premiums that a salesperson leaves with prospects or customers to remind them of the product or service.

link A function that takes a user, with just one click, from one page on the Web to another.

list price The price regularly quoted to customers before applying discounts. These are usually the prices printed on dealer lists, invoices, price tags, catalogs, or dealer purchase orders.

logo A distinctive company symbol that helps create an image or brand.

market research Data pertaining to customers within a market segment.

market segment A group of actual or potential customers who can be expected to respond in approximately the same way to a given offer.

market segmentation The act of dividing up a market into distinct groups of buyers to better target your marketing efforts.

market share The percentage of total buyers for a product or service who choose to buy from your company.

marketing audit (or assessment) An analysis of the company's current marketplace, current marketing capabilities, and potential opportunities.

marketing consultant An individual or firm who by training and experience is qualified to help a company with its marketing efforts.

marketing integration The coordination of all marketing strategies so they work together to establish maximum impact in the market.

marketing mix The combination of all elements used to market a product or service. These include product, price, place (distribution), and promotion.

marketing plan The annual planning document that sets the marketing direction for a product, service, or company. It spells out the strategies, tactics, time lines, and budgetary details for accomplishing the marketing objectives.

marketing strategy(ies) The broad directional thrusts a business uses to achieve its marketing goals. Characterized by broad decisions concerning price, product, distribution, and/or promotional issues.

marketing tactics The executable elements or actual steps the marketers will take to achieve their objectives and strategies.

medium (pl. media) A type of publication or communications tool that conveys news, entertainment, and advertising to an audience. Examples include newspapers, television, magazines, radio, billboards, and the Internet.

metrics The measurements a marketer uses to analyze and assess a marketing effort.

mission statement A formal statement of the reason a company or organization exists.

niche marketing A way of finding a special product that appeals to only one group and selling that product very profitably only to that group, ignoring others.

offer What you offer, as an inducement to buy, in your direct mail (e.g., buy one, get one free).

opt-in vehicles Any marketing vehicle in any marketing campaign where buyers explicitly request to be included in the campaign.

order(s) The point where a customer agrees to exchange money for goods or services provided by a company. Can also be called a purchase order.

planning The process of predetermining a course or courses of action based on assumptions about future conditions or trends.

position The perception that a marketer attempts to convey about a brand and its benefits vis-à-vis the competition.

pretest The testing of a research survey (or, for that matter, any marketing program) before launching it in order to fine-tune the survey administration.

price The amount of money asked for in the transfer of products and services from the provider(s) to the consumer(s).

pricing strategy Pricing for long-term advantage rather than short-term profits.

product A manufactured good that possesses objective and subjective characteristics that are manipulated to maximize the item's appeal to consumers. In general, appeals are directed at satisfying people's basic needs for such things as health, security, wealth, love, or accomplishment.

promotion All forms of communication other than advertising that call attention to products and services, typically by adding extra value to the purchase. Includes temporary discounts, allowances, premium offers, coupons, contests, and rebates.

prospects Identified consumers—individuals or companies—who show good potential for buying a company's products or services and have made contact with a company. Also called *buyers*.

psychographics Shared attitudes or behaviors of population groups.

publicity Information with news value used to promote a product, service, or idea in the media.

qualitative In research, verbatim or verbal feedback achieved through nonscientific and nonprojectable research.

quantitative In research, measurable, projectable data used to help determine needs or wants.

rationale A logical reasoning for choosing a strategy.

reach The total number of individuals or companies that are exposed to a marketing vehicle.

recency A term for how recent a person has bought from your company. It is well established that people who have bought most recently are more likely to buy from you again on your next promotion.

referral Name of a prospective customer who was acquired from a current customer or other third party.

search engine Online software that helps users locate information and other sites on the Internet.

seasonality The variations in sales or response that are attributable to the change in season. For example, hot cocoa sales are much stronger in winter, while iced-tea-mix sales are stronger in the summer.

segment A portion of a list or file selected on the basis of a special set of characteristics.

self-mailer A direct-mail piece, such as a postcard or tabbed newsletter, which does not require an envelope or wrapper for mailing.

service Any activity provided by a person or company to another person or company that is intangible. Services can be provided separately from products or they can be bundled together with products.

strategy(ies) Any broad plan(s) for achieving goals or objectives.

suspects Identified consumers—individuals or companies—who show good potential for buying a company's products or services but have not yet made contact with a company. See *prospect*.

tactics The actual programs and techniques used to accomplish a strategy.

target market The defined group of consumers that a marketer considers to be prime prospects (i.e., most likely to purchase).

target marketing Where different products, pricing, distribution methods, and promotions are developed to meet consumers' varying needs and preferences.

test market Trial market for a new product, service, offer, or other marketing effort.

time line A specific action plan, laid out in a visual way, that lists the various tactics a company will pursue and the subsequent deadlines.

touchpoint Any place where a business comes into contact with its customers or prospects.

trademark The name, phrase, logo, image, or combination of images of a product or brand claimed as owned by a marketer. Often marked as ™ if the mark has been applied for and ® if it has been registered. The term is often used to include service marks, which apply to businesses providing services as opposed to selling products.

trial The initial customer use of a product or service. Either given away free or sold at a nominal price to gain customer experience with the brand.

trial offer The offer to a consumer to try a product for a stated period of time before deciding whether or not to purchase.

unique selling proposition The specific, unique benefit that differentiates your product or service from all your competitors. Made famous by Rosser Reeves, an ad giant of the 1950s.

URL Universal Resource Locator. The text address that allows users to find a particular Web site or Web page. The links on Web pages also consist of URLs, which are embedded in the HTML code on the page. A URL contains a domain name followed by the file path to a particular file on that domain's Web server.

value-added Any promotional, product, or service technique that seeks to add value to the product.

Web page A page in a Web document. Unlike printed pages, a Web page may be just a few words long or it may include thousands of words, images, and other content.

weakness A shortcoming of a company that potentially could place it at a competitive disadvantage.

word-of-mouth advertising Getting satisfied customers to recommend the product or service to friends, family, coworkers, or anyone else they're familiar with.

Marketing Books

Alsop, Ronald J. *The 18 Immutable Laws of Corporate Reputation.* New York: Free Press, 2004.

Bangs, David H. *The Market Planning Guide.* Chicago: Dearborn Trade Publishing, 2002.

Barrett, Fred. *Names That Sell: How to Create Great Names for Your Company, Product, or Service.* Portland, OR: Alder Press, 1995.

Bayan, Richard. *Words That Sell.* Lincolnwood, IL: Contemporary Books, 1984.

Beckwith, Harry. *Selling the Invisible: A Field Guide to Modern Marketing.* New York: Warner Books, 1997.

Blake, George Burroughs, and Nancy Blake-Bohne. *Crafting the Perfect Name.* Chicago: Probus Publishing Company, 1991.

Blankenship, A.B., and George Edward Breen. *State of the Art Marketing Research.* New York: McGraw-Hill, 1998.

Bly, Robert. *Selling Your Services.* New York: Owl Books, 1991.

Breen, George Edward, and A.B. Blankenship. *Do-It-Yourself Marketing Research.* New York: McGraw-Hill, 1991.

Caples, John. *Tested Advertising Methods.* Upper Saddle River, NJ: Prentice-Hall, 1998.

Cialdini, Robert. *Influence: The Psychology of Persuasion.* New York: HarperCollins, 1998.

Charmasson, Henri. *The Name Is the Game: How to Name a Company or Product.* Burr Ridge, IL: Dow Jones-Irwin, 1988.

——. *The Name's the Thing: Creating the Perfect Name for your Company or Product.* New York: AMACOM, 1991.

Dolan, Robert J., and Hermann Simon. *Power Pricing: How Managing Price Transforms the Bottom Line.* New York: The Free Press, 1996.

Godin, Seth. *Unleashing the Idea Virus.* New York: Simon & Schuster, 2002.

——. *The Big Red Fez: How to Make Any Web Site Better.* New York: Free Press, 2002.

——. *All Marketers Are Liars.* New York: Portfolio, 2005.

Gray, Daniel. *Looking Good on the Web.* Scottsdale, AZ: The Coriolis Group, 1999.

Harding, Ford. *Rain Making: The Professional's Guide to Attracting New Clients.* Holbrook, MA: Bob Adams, Inc., 1994.

Kennedy, Daniel S. *The Ultimate Marketing Plan.* Avon, MA: Adams Media Corporation, 2000.

Kotler, Philip. *Kotler on Marketing: How to Create, Win, and Dominate Markets.* New York: Free Press, 1999.

——. *Marketing Management,* 11th Edition. Upper Saddle River, NJ: Prentice-Hall, 2002.

Krug, Steve. *Don't Make Me Think: A Common Sense Approach to Web Usability.* Indianapolis, IN: New Riders Press, 2005.

Kuegler, Thomas. *Web Advertising and Marketing.* Premier Press, 2000.

Levinson, Jay Conrad, and Seth Godin. *The Guerrilla Marketing Handbook.* New York: Houghton Mifflin, 1994.

Levinson, Jay Conrad. *Guerrilla Marketing Weapons.* New York: Plume, 1990.

Locke, Christopher, et al. *The Cluetrain Manifesto: The End of Business as Usual.* New York: Perseus Books, 2001.

Nagel, Thomas T., and Reed Holden. *The Strategy and Tactics of Pricing.* Upper Saddle River, NJ: Prentice-Hall, 2002.

Nielsen, Jakob, and Marie Tahir. *Homepage Usability: 50 Websites Deconstructed.* Berkeley, CA: New Riders Press, 2001.

Nielsen, Jakob. *Designing Web Usability: The Practice of Simplicity.* Berkeley, CA: New Riders Press, 1999.

Popyk, Bob. *Here's My Card: How to Network Using Your Business Card to Actually Create More Business.* Renaissance Books, 2000.

Porter, Michael. *Competitive Advantage: Creating and Sustaining Superior Performance.* New York: Free Press, 1998.

——. *Competitive Strategy: Techniques for Analyzing Industries and Competitors.* New York: Free Press, 1998.

Ries, Al, and Jack Trout. *Positioning: The Battle for Your Mind.* Burr Ridge, IL: McGraw-Hill, 2000.

Ries, Al, and Laura Ries. *The 22 Immutable Laws of Branding.* New York: HarperCollins, 2000.

Rohr, Ellen. *How Much Should I Charge? Pricing Basics for Making Money Doing What You Love.* Springfield, MO: Maxrohr, 1999.

Schmitt, Bernd, and Alex Simonson. *Marketing Aesthetics: The Strategic Management of Brands, Identity and Image.* New York: Free Press, 1997.

Seybold, Patricia B., and Ronni T. Marshak. *The Customer Revolution.* New York: Crown Business, 2001.

Shenk, David. *Data Smog: Surviving the Information Glut.* San Francisco: HarperSanFrancisco, 1998.

Sterne, Jim. *World Wide Web Marketing: Integrating the Web into Your Marketing Strategy*, 3rd Edition. New York: John Wiley & Sons, 2001.

Sullivan, Jenny. *Creative Solutions: Brochures: Making a Strong Impression.* Gloucester, MA: Rockport Publishers, 2004.

Trout, Jack. *The Power of Simplicity: A Management Guide to Cutting Through the Nonsense and Doing Things Right.* New York: McGraw-Hill, 2000.

Trout, Jack, with Steve Rivkin. *Differentiate or Die: Survival in Our Era of Killer Competition.* New York: John Wiley & Sons, 2001.

Vitale, Joseph G. *AMA Complete Guide to Small Business Advertising.* Chicago: NTC Business Books, 1994.

Weinstein, Art. *Handbook of Market Segmentation: Strategic Targeting for Business and Technology Firms.* New York: Haworth Press, 2004.

Wheildon, Colin. *Type & Layout: Are you Communicating or Just Making Pretty Shapes?* Mentone, Victoria, Australia: Worsley Press, 2005.

Williams, Phil. *Naming Your Business: How to Create Effective Trade Names, Trademarks, and Service Marks to Attract Customers, Protect Your Goodwill and Reputation, and Stay out of Court!* Oak Park, IL: P. Gaines Publishing Company, 1991.

Young, Davis. *Building Your Company's Good Name: How to Create & Protect the Reputation Your Organization Wants & Deserves.* New York: AMACOM Publishing, 1996.

Yudkin, Marsha. *Persuading on Paper: The Complete Guide to Writing Copy That Pulls in Business.* West Conshohocken, PA: Infinity Publishing, 2002.

Zimmerman, Jan. *Marketing on the Internet.* Gulf Breeze, FL: Maximum Press, 2000.

Top Ten Marketing Web Sites

1. MarketingSherpa.com *(www.marketingsherpa.com)*. Undoubtedly one of the best marketing sites online, MarketingSherpa, Inc., is a research firm that publishes case studies, benchmark data, and how-to information for market-

ing, advertising, and public relations professionals. Sign up for any of its numerous e-mails and you'll stay up-to-the-minute informed.

2. MarketingProfs.com *(www.marketingprofs.com)*. This online publishing company specializes in "Providing both strategic and tactical post-MBA marketing know-how to Internet and off-line marketing professionals in medium and large corporations, through a combination of provocative articles and commentary." Some of the better content *is* premium content, available only if you pay.

3. MarketingExperiments.com *(www.marketingexperiments.com)*. Marketing experiments is an online laboratory with a five-word mission statement: *To discover what really works.* The lab tests every conceivable marketing method on the Internet and then reports back, through e-mails, on the outcomes. If you have a significant online presence, and are committed to the concept of testing, bookmark this one.

4. ClickZNetwork.com *(www.clickz.com)*. The ClickZ Network is the largest resource of interactive marketing news, information, commentary, advice, opinion, research, and reference in the world, online or offline. From search to e-mail, technology to trends, its mission is to help interactive marketers perform their jobs better.

5. EmergeMarketing.com *(www.emergemarketing.com)*. Okay, I'm biased because this is my site. But it does feature many free articles covering a host of marketing topics such as: *The 5 Most Common Marketing Mistakes (and How to Avoid Them), How to Successfully Market Your Website,* and *Cut Bickering Between Sales and Marketing with These Tips.* You'll also find my *Smart Marketing* blog, a glossary with 300+ marketing definitions, and a sign-up for my e-newsletter *Marketing Tips and Tools.*

6. HighRankings.com *(www.highrankings.com)*. Jill Whalen, owner of High Rankings.com since 1995, is a real expert in search-engine optimization techniques. Her site contains a number of excellent articles and free resources. To me, the most valuable resource at this site is her forum, located at *www.highrankings.com/forum,* where you'll get hands-on advice for almost any search topic from some world-renowned experts.

7. MarketingTips.com (Internet Marketing Center) *(www.marketingtips.com)*. This site, begun by the late Internet guru Corey Rudl, is a great place to start if you want to increase your Web site's bottom-line contribution. Not only are there great articles and information, but the site also sells indispensable tools, including the information-packed course, "The Insider's Secrets to Marketing Your Business on the Internet." There is also a complete e-mail management software package called Mailloop, an affiliate tracking soft-

ware program called AssocTRAC, and an eBook publishing tool called eBook Pro.

8. Marketing.About.com *(http://marketing.about.com)*. According to Nielsen NetRatings, About.com is a top 15 Web property used by one out of every five people on the Internet. Granted, this site is only one of the many content channels offered, but I still think it provides a nuts-and-bolts approach to common marketing issues facing business owners.

9. MarketingPower.com *(www.marketingpower.com)*. The American Marketing Association's (AMA) Web site, MarketingPower.com supplies marketing professionals and AMA members with information, products, and services to help them succeed in their jobs and careers.

10. WebMarketingToday.com *(www.wilsonweb.com* or *http://webmarketingto-day.com)*. The site is known as WebMarketingToday.com but uses either of these addresses. Dr. Ralph Wilson has built quite an impressive site, indeed, with more than 2,200 pages and 15,000 links to resources on e-commerce and Web marketing. There are lots of resources to take advantage of here.